DRAGONS

Also by Diana Cooper
and published by Hay House

Books

The Archangel Guide to the Animal World (2017)
The Archangel Guide to Enlightenment and Mastery (2016)
The Archangel Guide to Ascension (2015)
Venus: A Diary of a Puppy and Her Angel (2014)

Oracle Card Decks

Archangel Animal Oracle Cards (2019)
Dragon Oracle Cards (2017)

CDs and Audio Downloads

The Archangel Guide to Enlightenment and Mastery (2016)
The Archangel Guide to Ascension (2015)

Your Celestial Guardians

DIANA COOPER

HAY HOUSE
Carlsbad, California • New York City
London • Sydney • New Delhi

Published in the United Kingdom by:
Hay House UK Ltd, The Sixth Floor, Watson House,
54 Baker Street, London W1U 7BU
Tel: +44 (0)20 3927 7290; Fax: +44 (0)20 3927 7291; www.hayhouse.co.uk

Published in the United States of America by:
Hay House Inc., PO Box 5100, Carlsbad, CA 92018-5100
Tel: (1) 760 431 7695 or (800) 654 5126; Fax: (1) 760 431 6948 or (800) 650 5115
www.hayhouse.com

Published in Australia by:
Hay House Australia Ltd, 18/36 Ralph St, Alexandria NSW 2015
Tel: (61) 2 9669 4299; Fax: (61) 2 9669 4144; www.hayhouse.com.au

Published in India by:
Hay House Publishers India, Muskaan Complex, Plot No.3, B-2,
Vasant Kunj, New Delhi 110 070
Tel: (91) 11 4176 1620; Fax: (91) 11 4176 1630; www.hayhouse.co.in

A catalogue record for this book is available from the British Library.

Tradepaper ISBN: 978-1-4019-7001-7
E-book ISBN: 978-1-78817-168-7

10 9 8 7 6 5 4 3 2 1

Printed in the United States of America

Contents

Introduction

I love the dragons and have especially enjoyed writing this book. As I have worked with these magnificent beings they have really helped me to grow spiritually. Again and again I have been bowled over by the information they have given me. I am constantly reminded that we live in an amazing universe.

I tuned in to most of the dragons I include in this book when I was creating my *Dragon Oracle Cards,* but for this project they have given me much more information about themselves and their work. Each time I sat down to write, a dragon would approach and a stream of light would be downloaded into my mind. This has happened much more powerfully than for any of my other books. Also new dragons have stepped forward and asked to be included.

I have written about the dragons who came to me for this book but there are many others, so be open to any that appear to you. As the consciousness of the planet rises more high-frequency dragons will be attracted to Earth to help with our transition to the new Golden Age.

Being a Virgo I usually start at the beginning and write each chapter as I have mapped it out. Not with the dragons! Each time I powered up my laptop one would be with me and I just had to write about that one.

On one occasion I had been thinking about spiritual community and decided that I would focus on the orange dragons. But these wise etheric beings had other ideas. A black and shining white dragon from Pluto nudged in and hassled me until I agreed to let go of my preconceived intention and tune in to him. The dragons made it quite clear that I was in service to them until this book was finished. They rather reminded me of my dog Venus, who is very clear about the attention she is due!

I have divided the book into four categories of dragons, though they all have equal importance and all are in service. They just have different tasks. I introduce the beautiful Lemurian dragons and how they offer us so much help in our everyday lives. Then we meet the fifth- to seventh-dimensional dragons who expand our consciousness and our spiritual path. In the section about the dragons who work with the archangels and masters, they show us about the wonderful way they cooperate with and support the angels and masters, so that they all work together for our happiness and ascension, raising our vibration to the level of Light.

I feel particularly attuned to the galactic dragons and especially enjoy their presence when outside looking at a starry night sky. Some of these amazing creatures are helping us with DNA repatterning, others taking us into different stargates to other universes. Most are connecting us to the wisdom held in the planets. I had some really powerful downloads of light when doing the visualization journeys they gave me. I hope you do too.

As you read this book and tune in to dragon frequencies, you may want to become a Dragon Master – one who can command the dragon forces. Of course, you may be one already, thanks to work you have done in this and other lives.

The dragons remind us that the journey to dragon mastery is threefold.

First, develop both feminine and masculine dragon qualities, so that you are balanced at all times. Feminine dragon qualities are being kind, caring, loving, patient, healing and open-hearted and hopeful, among others. Masculine dragon qualities include strength, power, mental and emotional control, determination, courage and the ability to make clear decisions, among others.

Second, master the elements.

Third, stay aligned to your truth with power at all times.

The dragons will respect you and work with you, so that you become a beacon of light.

The dragons want this book to open you up to their presence, so that they can serve you while you are on Earth. They can help you in so many ways. As with the angels, all you have to do is ask!

To download images of some of the dragons who have stepped forward to be included in this book, just follow the instructions on page 289.

PART I

Dragons and Their History

Introduction

Dragons are wise beings of the angelic realms. They are on different wavelengths from angels but they work together for the highest good, each performing their allotted tasks.

Dragons are extremely sage, courageous, open-hearted beings who have been serving our planet from its inception. They have a great affinity with and love for humans and for Earth. If one becomes your companion, it supports you and the bond is unbreakable. Your dragon will return to you whenever you need it.

They watch over us and they guard the treasures of our world. These are the caches of wisdom held in certain crystals, rocks and trees, the magic hidden in some caves, the songs of the mountains or the mysteries of the natural world.

They can create matter and deconstruct it. In other words, they can physically materialize and they can destroy. The angels hold the vision while the dragons manifest it.

Like all beings of the angelic realms they will do your bidding as long as it is for the highest good but only if you ask.

Chapter 1

Who Are the Dragons?

Dragons are elementals. This means they do not have all four elements as humans do. They can have earth, air, fire or water or a combination of any two or three of them.

To put them in context:

- Angels and unicorns are of the element air.
- Fairies, sylphs and esaks (new elementals recently arrived on Earth from another universe to purify it for the new Golden Age) are air elementals.
- Goblins, gnomes and elves are earth elementals.
- Mermaids, undines (water nymphs) and kyhils (more new elementals recently arrived from another universe to purify the Earth for the new Golden Age), are water elementals.
- Salamanders are fire elementals.
- Imps, pixies, fauns and many others have more than one element.

All elementals are of the angelic kingdom but have different roles and operate on different frequency bands. It is becoming easier to tune in to their wavelengths as we raise our vibrational level.

Dragons, angels, unicorns and nature spirits do not have free will. Only humans have that. The angelic role is to serve God and to help people, animals and the natural world.

Air Elementals

All air elementals inspire you, blow away the old and bring in higher energies.

Air dragons are always ready to clear etheric cobwebs from your home or your mind and to create a higher vortex of energy to replace them. They can breathe fire.

Fire Elementals

All fire elementals burn away and transmute lower energies so that the new can come in.

Fire dragons are extremely powerful. If you ask they will create an etheric wall of fire round you, your home or your loved ones for protection and to clear energies that impact on you.

Earth Elementals

Earth elementals look after the soil and keep the land clear of lower frequencies.

Earth dragons maintain ley lines and clear negative energies under the surface of earth. They can breathe fire.

Water Elementals

Water elementals keep the energy of love flowing.

Water dragons are smooth like snakes and they carry the love of the universe wherever they go. Water is everywhere, not just in lakes and oceans but in the atmosphere and in the cells of our bodies. These great open-hearted creatures move fluidly, spreading Christ light throughout the universe. They cannot breathe fire.

Dragons' Shape

The Intergalactic Council, (a body of 12 mighty beings who take decisions for the evolution of Earth), under guidance from Source, chose the reptilian shape for dragons so that they could easily glide and slide through the dimensions and enter confined spaces that other beings could not access.

They have long served in this and other universes and their hearts are so bright with love that they have developed etheric wings. Their wings become more ethereal as their frequency rises.

Tuning in to Dragons

Dragons are part of our ancient history, so knowing them is encoded into our memory banks. Now that the dragons are returning to help us, this memory is becoming stronger in the collective consciousness, so it is becoming easier to tune in to them. The moment you think about a dragon or any ethereal being, it comes to you. So, the more you think or talk about dragons, the closer they are. For many people this trust in the presence of dragons is enough.

Tuning in to their wavelength is like finding a radio programme. The more you fine-tune the connection with meditation, visualization, prayer and all kinds of spiritual work, the clearer your communication becomes.

I often think people have unrealistic expectations of seeing a dragon in glorious technicolour and clearly hearing what it says. This may be possible for those who are clairvoyant and clairaudient as a result of many lifetimes of spiritual dedication. However, most people just have occasional flashes of seeing and hearing or they have psychic impressions and this is enough.

Those who work with claircognizance or knowing will receive downloads and whispers. They have to lower their frequency to see clairvoyantly, so I always suggest that people trust their intuition, for what they receive is perfect for them.

Dragons in the Clouds

Dragons are usually very busy and active but occasionally one may rest in the sky as it watches over a project. As with all beings or objects that are at a different frequency from that of our planet, condensation gathers round it. This is when you see a dragon shape – or an angel, unicorn or flying saucer – in the sky. Even when the being has left, its outline can be seen as a cloud in the sky that gradually disperses.

A Resumé of Dragon History

Here is a brief resumé of the history of the dragons. In the following chapters I expand on their history, their role and how we can work with them to restore our planet to its rightful place in the universe.

1. Dragons were present at Angala, the birth of Earth, and helped with its formation.

2. In the Golden Age of Petranium, the ancient civilization that seeded Africa, dragons worked with crystals to keep the portals

to the stars clear so that the people could access stellar wisdom. They ensured water was in the right place for irrigation.

3. In the Golden Age of Mu, the dragons formed the links between Earth, Sirius, Neptune, the Pleiades and Orion and protected the blue-aquamarine flame of wisdom held in the Hollow Centre (an energetic space or cosmic chakra) of each one. The beings of Mu loved the mountains and kept the songs of the mountains in tune. The dragons still protect the mountains and their music.

4. The etheric beings of the Golden Age of Lemuria so loved Earth that at the end of the civilization they created liquid crystals containing the wisdom of the stars. These were specifically intended to help our planet during the period from 2012 to 2032. The dragons helped to place this liquid light into seams in the rock, so that Lemurian crystals could reappear to assist us now.

5. In preparation for the Golden Era of Atlantis, dragons formed the Hill of Poseidon on which the temple that housed the Great Crystal was built. (The Great Crystal held information that high priests and priestesses downloaded to individual temple crystals.) Throughout this era they diligently protected the Great Crystal and kept the people, the continent and the portals to the stars energetically clear. And at the end of Atlantis they were offered promotion to the fifth dimension as a reward for their great service, but they declined because they said humanity would need their help after 2012. This spiritual sacrifice is now being rewarded.

6. When the Temple of Poseidon collapsed and the Great Crystal fell into the centre of the Bermuda Triangle, the water dragons

continued to protect it. Not only was it an advanced computer and generator powered by Source energy but it was an intergalactic portal. The dragons guard all beings who travel through the portal.

7. At the current time, more and more high-frequency dragons and intergalactic ones are returning to play their part in the ascension of Earth.

Chapter 2

Dragons and the Birth of Earth

Aeons ago, Source, in consultation with the Intergalactic Council for this universe, decided to create our unique planet. The vision was held in the mind of God while the dragons took the concept and helped to create the physical earth and rock.

Fire and air dragons were needed for the explosion of energy that formed the planet and so they duly arrived for this purpose. Earth dragons provided the elemental energies for the physical manifestation of Earth.

The water dragons enabled the Christ light, golden-white energy of pure love, to flow round and through the planet as it was birthed. As dragons circled the world with loving protection, tier upon tier of golden angels formed round it, gloriously singing the divine vision for Earth. And so Earth was born into a golden cocoon and the first Golden Age on this planet, known as Angala, began.

Angala Is an Eternal Moment

Time is not linear as we understand it.

When you are in a third-dimensional reality, time appears to go very slowly. The usual example of this is watching that proverbial kettle taking a long time to boil. If you are impatiently waiting, time does indeed appear to elongate. This is only because impatient waiting is a third-dimensional, low-frequency quality. If you have a 10-minute wait for transport when you are cold, wet and miserable, it seems to drag interminably. If you are happy and it is sunny, that 10 minutes goes by in a flash.

Happiness, love, peace, beauty and balance are some of the fifth-dimensional qualities and when you are in one of these states, time appears to accelerate.

The higher your frequency, the more quickly it seems to pass. At a twelfth-dimensional frequency all time is simultaneous. From that perspective there is no past or future. Everything is now.

Angala was conceived in the mind of God, at a twelfth-dimensional frequency when elongated time condenses to one instant. Therefore, it is an eternal moment. You can access an Angala moment for the beginning of any special project.

If you start a new business, relationship or anything else in an Angala moment, you are automatically calling in the impetus of the birth of Earth to thrust it forward. Consciously or unconsciously you are surrounding your vision with singing angels and blessing it with dragon power and unicorn light.

Angala may only have lasted a fraction of a second in Earth time but it blesses us for ever.

Exercise to Access an Angala Moment for a New Idea or Project

1. Find a space where you can be quiet and undisturbed.
2. Close your eyes and centre yourself.
3. Imagine golden roots going down from your feet into the earth below you.
4. Think of the birthing of Earth.
5. See the fire, air and earth dragons creating the great sphere of our planet.
6. Watch the water dragons flowing and undulating around it, pouring Christ light around it until Earth is in a cocoon of golden love.
7. Be aware of the angels all around it, blessing it and singing the divine vision for the planet.
8. Now project the idea you want to birth into the centre of your picture.
9. Know that the dragons and angels are helping to birth your dream.
10. Thank them and open your eyes.

Chapter 3

Dragons at the Time of Petranium, the Golden Age of Africa

The second Golden Age on Earth was in Africa at the time of Petranium, the ancient civilization that seeded the African races. Africa is overseen by Afra, a seventh-dimensional illumined being, who is a Dragon Master.

During the Golden Age the entire continent of Africa was covered in bright verdant vegetation. The soil was rich.

At the start of this Golden Age the beings who inhabited it were etheric and seventh dimensional. They accessed minerals by merging their energy with that of the soil and then spreading the ores where they were most needed for the land. Cooperating with the dragons, the beings of Petranium were able to move the clouds and cause rain to fall where it was required.

Connection with the Stars

The crystals at that time were awake and beamed light out to the stars. The dragons worked with the 'people' of that time to ensure they were totally connected to the stars through the crystals. They also helped to keep the portals clear.

It was only when this connection diminished that the frequency of the inhabitants lowered and they became physical. The food they ate and the hot climate determined the black colour of their skin. They all worked on the blue ray of healing and communication.

South Africa

South Africa is the solar plexus chakra of Earth. Your personal solar plexus chakra, when it is third dimensional, absorbs the fear around you. It is only when you become fifth dimensional that your solar plexus chakra transmutes all fear and becomes a glorious, vibrant, radiant golden ball of knowledge, true self-worth and wisdom. Because Earth is the solar plexus of this universe, the fear of the universe passes through South Africa. It is this that holds the whole of Africa back.

The dragons are patiently waiting to cleanse the crystals and light them up so that they reconnect with the awesome knowledge they hold from all over the universes. When this happens, South Africa will become a radiant, golden place, where all the inhabitants have true self-worth and wisdom. They will be able to illuminate the planet, access minerals without damaging the structure of the Earth, control the waters and direct the clouds so that rain falls in right places. The information held within the crystals means that Africa is one of the places that is key to the future irrigation of the planet when it will be much needed.

The Original Ones

Some of the original beings of Petranium remain in their etheric bodies at a seventh-dimensional frequency in order to guide and help Africa. Currently, those who sense their presence are afraid of them but as the vibration rises people will listen to them again.

Planetary Service Work

For this work, you will need to draw or print a map of Africa. If you wish to do so, colour it in to energize it. Now light a candle and dedicate it to the healing of Africa. Next, find a pebble or use a quartz crystal if you have one, and activate it by holding it above the flame. Ask the dragons to work with your intention of healing Africa and place the pebble or crystal on the map. Put the map on your altar or in a safe place where you can continue to work with the crystal for a week.

Visualization to Clear and Light up the Crystals of Africa

1. If you have one, hold a quartz crystal in your hand.
2. Find a space where you can be quiet and undisturbed.
3. Close your eyes and centre yourself.
4. Imagine golden roots going down from your feet into the earth below you.
5. Call thousands of earth dragons to swirl through the land under Africa to clear old energies.
6. Send thousands of water dragons to spread the Christ light in the waters of Africa.
7. Ask thousands of fire dragons to burn up third-dimensional vibrations on the surface.
8. Invoke thousands of air dragons to blow away stuck energy and inspire the people.
9. Invite dragons and angels to clear and cleanse the crystals.
10. See the dragons lighting up those crystals and reconnecting them to the stars.
11. Visualize the wisdom of the stars falling as blessings into the minds of receptive people on Earth.
12. Thank the dragons and open your eyes.

Chapter 4

Dragons and the Third Golden Age: Mu

The beings of Mu, a civilization that preceded Lemuria, were etheric and never took physical form. Founders of a Golden Age in the Pacific, they vibrated at a fourth-dimensional frequency and it was only when the great Illumined 11th-dimensional Lord Voosloo arrived to overlight them that the civilization took a great leap and ascended into the fifth dimension.

Protecting the Harmonies of the Mountains

The tune of each of their songs depends on the metals, minerals, crystals and gems found within the mountains and the energies that they have absorbed. The inhabitants of Mu had a particular affinity with the mountains and the dragons protected the harmonies that they emitted at that time. They still protect the great mountains of our planet. However, many of them are now out of tune and it is time to cleanse them and bring them back into harmony again.

Cooperating with Ascension

The beings of Mu had a great love for our planet Earth as well as for Neptune, Orion, Sirius and the Pleiades. These five planets, stars and constellations have always had a special relationship. They are now all ascending and help to hold each other's energy so that we can all rise together fully into the fifth dimension.

The beings of Mu cooperated with the golden dragons of Earth, the aquamarine dragons of Neptune, the pure white dragons of Orion, the green-gold dragons of Sirius and the blue healing dragons of the Pleiades to keep the links between us all strong.

Earth, Neptune, Orion, Sirius and the Pleiades each has a Hollow Centre, within which is an aquamarine-blue flame of wisdom, love and healing. This is formed from the light of Archangel Michael and Angel Mary in perfect masculine–feminine balance.

The beings of Mu still hold the wisdom of the other four stellar connections within an etheric Metatron Cube in Hollow Earth and this is protected by many dragons, overseen by the crystal yellow dragons.

Visualization to Help the Dragons Return the Wisdom of the Golden Age of Mu

1. Find a space where you can be quiet and undisturbed.
2. Close your eyes and centre yourself.
3. Visualize yourself standing within the dragon portal at the top of a sacred snow-covered mountain in Andorra, Spain. Feel the pure energy.

4. Imagine golden roots going from your feet into the earth, down through the mountain into the centre of Hollow Earth.
5. Be aware of the golden dragons spinning through your roots into the blue aquamarine flame in the centre of the Great Pyramid of Hollow Earth. See the flame light up.
6. Then look up and see the blue dragons of the Pleiades flying up to the blue aquamarine flame in the centre of the Pleiades. See the flame light up.
7. Next, imagine the aquamarine dragons of Neptune flying up to the blue aquamarine flame in the centre of Neptune. See the flame light up.
8. Visualize the pure white dragons of Orion flying up to the blue aquamarine flame in the centre of Orion. See the flame light up.
9. Finally, imagine the green-gold dragons of Sirius flying up to the blue aquamarine flame in the centre of Sirius. See the flame light up.
10. Ask the dragons to keep linking Earth, the Pleiades, Sirius, Orion and Neptune and watch them making the connections.
11. Ask the golden dragons of Earth and the dragons of the Pleiades, Sirius, Orion and Neptune to make your inner connections.
12. Be aware of the angels singing the world into harmony and let the vibrations flow over you.
13. Open your eyes and know that you and the dragons have served the universe.

Chapter 5

Dragons and the Fourth Golden Age: Lemuria

Lemuria was the golden civilization before Atlantis and beings from many universes arrived to take part in the new experience. At that time, they did not have physical bodies and were androgynous. They were not individuals but were like a fifth-dimensional harmonizing force that drifted through the universe, touching and healing places where they were needed. They were always accompanied and protected by an army of Lemurian dragons.

Loving the Earth

The Lemurians particularly loved Earth. They treasured trees and the entire world of nature found here.

They drew love and light from Source through the Cosmic Heart into the centre of Hollow Earth. They also linked lovingly into the ascension stars, planets and constellations of Neptune, Orion, Sirius and the Pleiades.

Lemurian Crystals

Towards the end of their civilization, the Lemurians created their incredibly pure and powerful healing crystals. They did this by merging energy from Source and specific qualities from the auras of many stars, planets and Earth itself. The dragons physicalized this energy and eventually placed the liquid crystal in seams within Earth. From there it flowed into the ley lines and lit the planet up from inside. The Lemurians created these crystals specifically to help humanity through this current 20-year period before the start of the new Golden Age. They knew we would need their healing properties now. The dragons have protected the awesome Lemurian crystals ever since.

You can ask the crystals to open the door to the dragon kingdom for you, then you can call specific dragons to you, which are able to work with your energy. Through the dragon kingdom you can access the wisdom of Lemuria.

Protecting the Wisdom of Lemuria

The dragons protect the wisdom of Lemuria. Their greatest gift was their blazing, fully open hearts. They loved passionately and poured agape into the trees, mountains, rivers and creatures of this planet. Their love was unconditional and transcendent.

Another treasure they earned was oneness. They moved as one where they were needed. They shared everything, including their consciousness and focused it into a single vision, which was to heal and to spread unity. Lemurian healing energy, that is now encapsulated in their crystals, is pure and powerful.

They understood abundance consciousness and lived in the flow of giving and receiving in equal measure.

With wide-open hearts they intuitively felt for all sentient beings, including crystals, mountains and trees. Their love helped to hold the frequencies high.

This consciousness is part of the treasure of Lemuria, stored in Neptune and Hollow Earth, protected by the dragons. If you wish to tune in to it and absorb the wisdom, ask the dragons to help you to access it.

The Lemurian crystals are another part of their treasure. These are cosmic keys that enable you to open doors to esoteric knowledge and wisdom, that you are ready to access.

Hollow Earth

Hollow Earth is the seventh-dimensional chakra in the centre of the Earth, in which everything that has ever been on the surface is held in etheric form. If you enter the Lemurian section of Hollow Earth, you can go through a portal into the dragon kingdom to access the knowledge and wisdom of the dragons.

Mother Mary

Mother Mary, the great Ascended Master who was known as Ma Ra in Lemuria, overlit the era. She is normally associated with unicorns and is often seen with one, but the dragons worked with her in Lemuria and did her bidding at all times.

Visualization to Connect with the Dragons of Lemuria

1. Find a place where you can be quiet and undisturbed.
2. Light a candle to raise the vibration, if possible.
3. Close your eyes and relax.

4. Invoke Mother Mary to come to you and picture her placing you in a ball of gentle blue light.
5. Invite the Lemurian dragons to weave their loving energy round you.
6. One of them approaches you and you sit on its back.
7. You are flying with it to the portal of Lemuria, in Hawaii.
8. As you enter the portal you find the dragon is taking you down into Hollow Earth.
9. You are in a white gold world, full of Lemurian memories.
10. Your dragon takes you into another portal that leads to the dragon kingdom.
11. Be aware of thousands of dragons resting, waiting for the call to action on Earth.
12. One dragon is holding an etheric crystal encoded with both the wisdom of Lemuria and the wisdom of the dragons.
13. You take it respectfully and hold it to your third eye. Relax.
14. When you return it, know that one or more doors to esoteric wisdom have opened within you.
15. Your dragon takes you back to where you started.
16. Thank it and open your eyes.

Chapter 6

Dragons in Atlantis and the Present Time

When the Intergalactic Council decided to undertake the fifth and final experiment of the Golden Age of Atlantis, the dragons were called upon to fashion the land. They assisted in the creation of the Hill of Poseidon, where the High Priests and Priestesses created the Temple itself. Inside it was placed the Great Crystal, powered by pure Source energy.

The Great Crystal powered a Dome of high-frequency energy over the continent. This invisible barrier acted as a protective bubble so that nothing and no one could access, interfere or leave it. This era of Atlantis was a controlled experiment and the dragons did their part to help it succeed.

Throughout this time, they diligently protected the Great Crystal. They also kept the people, the continent and the portals to the stars energetically clear. And at the end of the era of Atlantis they were offered promotion to the fifth dimension as a reward for their great service, but they declined because they said humanity would need their help after 2012. What an incredible sacrifice!

When the experiment of Atlantis imploded and most of the continent was submerged under the ocean, the Great Crystal fell into the centre of the Bermuda Triangle. The water dragons took over the role of protecting it. Not only was it an advanced computer and generator powered by Source energy but it was also an intergalactic portal.

The dragons look after all beings who travel through the portal. For thousands of years, if anyone entered the Bermuda Triangle at a time when the Intergalactic Council was using the portal, that person went through a rapid interdimensional shift. They seemed to disappear. In fact, they were quickly taken by the dragons into another dimension, a different space where humans cannot see them. Like death, it is a soul decision to undergo this experience. It does not happen by chance.

Nowadays, the consciousness of humanity has risen so that the impact on people who enter the Bermuda Triangle is minimal.

The Harmonic Convergence of 1987

Between 16 and 17 August 1987 there was an exceptional alignment of planets in the Solar System. At that time there was a period of synchronized meditation and prayer throughout the world, known as the Harmonic Convergence. It was noted in the Mayan Calendar that it marked the beginning of the 25-year purification of Earth, leading up to the Cosmic Moment of 2012.

For me it was one of those extraordinary and magical times. With two friends I was sitting on a local hilltop as the Sun rose. I knew people who were meditating at every power spot in the area and we were linked by an invisible thread. The sunrise was one of the most glorious I have ever experienced and I think it was the first time I have ever felt lit up internally and externally. It marked a change in the world.

The energy was so profound that St Germain took a petition to Source on behalf of humanity for the return of the Violet Flame, which clears and transmutes lower energies. This had been withdrawn at the end of Atlantis. At that time, like any high-frequency energy in the hands of low-consciousness people, it had been misused. Now at last humanity was deemed ready to use it appropriately again to transmute that which no longer served. The Violet Flame of Transmutation was returned to us by St Germain and Archangel Zadkiel.

The Mahatma Energy, a pool of golden-white collective consciousness created by many great beings in Atlantis, was also returned to us at that time to raise our frequency and light up our chakra systems.

The Stargate of Lyra opened a crack and seventh-dimensional unicorns started to slip through it to Earth to connect with people who wanted to serve. And the fourth-dimensional dragons started to return.

The Cosmic Moment in 2012

At 11:11 a.m. precisely on 21 December 2012, the long-awaited Cosmic Moment occurred. Predicted as the end of time, in fact it marked the end of the 260,000-year period of Atlantis and started the 20-year transition to the new Golden Age of Aquarius, the sixth Golden Age on this planet, which commences in 2032.

At the Cosmic Moment, Source touched the heart centres of every sentient being on this planet, in this universe and throughout all the universes. It ignited the great movement of every universe to a higher frequency. Ascension began.

Thirty-three cosmic portals radiating Christ light started to open, as well as many others. The cosmic dragon portals of Lemuria, Andorra and Honolulu opened and huge numbers of fourth- and fifth-dimensional dragons poured in to help us. Dragon light returned.

What Happened in 2015

The Stargate of Lyra opened fully, allowing the golden-white dragons of Lyra, along with many seventh-dimensional unicorns and some incredible golden-horned, ninth-dimensional unicorns, to come to Earth. They travel here along a finger of Archangel Christiel's energy from Lyra through the Moon.

The water dragons released their protection round the Great Crystal of Atlantis, which rose once more. A fountain of light was sent out. Unfortunately, the Great Crystal was slightly out of alignment with the Helios, the Great Central Sun, so the light only illuminated part of the planet. As a result of the intervention of many lightworkers, it came fully into alignment in 2017 and is having a dramatic impact on the ascension of Earth.

More and more dragons are flooding here to help us prepare for the new Golden Age.

PART II

Fourth-dimensional Dragons

Introduction

The fourth-dimensional dragons, who are such wise big-hearted beings, are Lemurian and truly in service to humanity. They act as personal companions and assist us and the planet in very many ways.

Like all beings who were connected to Earth at the time of Lemuria, they hold a special love for humans, nature and our planet. They have a burning desire to help us ascend into the new Golden Age.

They are waiting to assist us to prepare energetically for the new golden energies coming in.

Chapter 1

How Fourth-dimensional Dragons Help Us

As with all beings of the angelic realms, fourth-dimensional dragons wish to help us but can only do so if we ask them to. They do not have free will. Their desire is the divine will. We humans, on the other hand, can choose what to do. If dragons, angels or any being of the illumined realms stepped in to help us without our permission, they could interfere with our karma and this is not permitted under spiritual law.

The wonderful dragons can delve into deep, dark vibrations that seventh-dimensional angels or unicorns cannot reach. They have the ability to burn up, blow away or wash out lower energies or obstacles in our path. They inspire, protect and ground us, and much more.

Quan Yin and Travel Through the Dimensions

Dragons enable us to travel through the dimensions. When you visit higher frequencies during meditation, a dragon has almost certainly joined you. It was these extraordinary beings who helped Quan Yin, the illumined Goddess-Master of Love and Compassion, to experience a 2000-year incarnation. Quan Yin was a great Dragon Master. In our current state of collective consciousness humans cannot maintain a physical body for so long. However, the dragons took her spirit and held it for her in the sixth and even seventh dimension. When required she would return fully into her physical fifth-dimensional body, where she would eat lightly to maintain her sheath of flesh, as we must all do.

Quan Yin worked with the fourth-dimensional dragons as well as those who exist in different frequency bands.

Quan Yin is often seen with her dragon draped round her shoulders from where it could leap into instant action whenever it was needed.

The Elements

The fourth-dimensional dragons contain one, two or three elements of air, earth, fire and water. This means they can be air, earth, fire or water dragons, or of mixed elements – fire and water, air and water, air and fire, earth and water, earth and fire or earth and air. Humans are made up of all four elements, but dragons are not.

Earth-and-air dragons are construction experts. The earth dragons in particular can move matter. You may see one resting on a hill that it helped to form thousands of years ago. Air dragons will blow matter from one place to another. They work with the wind and other air elementals. Fire dragons are transmuters. Water dragons work with the streams, rivers and oceans to move matter by eroding or depositing it according to the divine plan.

Meet the Dragons

If possible, create a space containing all four elements: for example, a lit candle for fire and to raise the energy; perhaps a feather or a balloon for air; a pebble, a crystal or a flower to represent earth; and a bowl or glass of water. Your attention to these details enables the dragons to draw near to you.

If you cannot do this, draw a flame, a feather, a stream and a flower or some similar symbol on a sheet of paper. You may like to place one symbol in each corner.

When you have prepared this, be aware that one or more dragons are with you. You may see, sense or feel their presence or simply trust that they are nearby.

Close your eyes for a moment to prepare your consciousness for their input. Again, you may or may not be knowingly aware of this input.

Then, open your eyes, take a sheet of paper and draw a dragon. It can be as simple, childlike or elaborate as you wish. This is not about being an artist. You should see my drawings – even my grandchildren laugh at them! Intuitively choose any hue or hues to colour in your picture. As you do this you are opening your channels to dragon energy.

If you are already connected to the dragons this process will deepen your link. And if you are just starting to know the dragons, this is the beginning of a magical journey.

Chapter 2

Earth Dragons

These dragons are earth elementals, who love the land and our planet. They can be all shades of brown from light tan to brown-black. Like pixies and gnomes, who are also earth elementals, they take care of, maintain, enrich and purify the soil.

Working with Ley Lines

Earth dragons also work with ley lines. These were originally known as dragon lines and earth dragons helped to construct them, so they have a special affinity with them and undertake to clear them.

One of their tasks is to move along the lines and free them when we ask them to do so. Because humans have caused the blockages with their negativity and wars, the dragons have to wait for us to ask them to transmute the lower frequencies. If they healed the Earth without being requested to do so, they would be interfering with the karma we have created. Our baser thoughts and actions leave a residue in the land and it is time now to release it and set our beloved planet free.

A physical body contains the essence – bad and good – of the being who inhabited it. If the person is buried, their mental, emotional and physical energetic imprint remains in the soil until it is cleared. This may be thousands of years. No one is perfect so it is a good idea to ask the dragons to go to burial grounds, however prehistoric and forgotten, to burn up and release the old. If bodies are buried on ley lines, the impact can be catastrophic. It may eventually cause problems further along the line: crops may wither; trees may die; children may sicken.

And it is not just ancient material that is blocking our ley lines. Imagine what is held in the earth under an abattoir, anywhere where factory farming takes place, under buildings where corrupt decisions are taken or horror films are made. Think of the energy under hospitals and prisons. Consider the density under schools where the soul missions of the children are not honoured or anywhere that people are unhappy.

Earth dragons can breathe out fire, so ask them to burn up lower frequencies that may be lurking under the surface of the Earth. Spiritual beings such as dragons, who surround and serve us, are amazing in their love, compassion, healing power and dedication. Asking them to help takes just a moment, but the result can be momentous for a home, a town, a country or the planet and all of its inhabitants.

A Personal Experience

I used to walk in some woodlands that I loved. But there was a certain part that I would hurry through because it made me shiver. Eventually I realized that it was the scene of an ancient battle where humans, horses and even dogs had been killed. Their fear and pain was still held at this place, so I called in the earth dragons as well as the Violet Flame of Transmutation to work under the land, clearing the anguish buried there. I also asked the angels to sing healing over the area and the unicorns to shower it with light. I did this every day for three weeks. After that I could walk happily through that section of the wood.

Gardening Help

Earth dragons love gardening and anything to do with the land. So, if you are planting flowers or trees, just send out a thought for an earth dragon to be with you. They can subtly help you to do the right thing or whisper to you to add manure or water or whatever is needed.

There were many dragons working to create the beautiful gardens of old that still inspire us. If you stand still and quietly in the centre of the beauty in such a place, you may well catch a glimpse of one.

Grounding Yourself

Earth dragons can also ground you. If you are an ungrounded person – in other words you often feel slightly off centre, have headaches or feel light-headed, sick or generally not with it – call in an earth dragon to help you. All you have to do is ask it to ground you. Then trust it is with you, helping to plant your roots into the earth. It may subtly influence you to go for a grounding walk or to eat different food. If your spirit easily comes out of your body (as mine did for the first 40 years of my life), the dragon may swirl over your head and push your spirit back into your body. It is such a relief to feel fully earthed.

Many humans become ungrounded because it is uncomfortable to deal with being on Earth in a physical body, so ask an earth dragon to help you manage your life.

Clearing Obstacles

Dragons are very good at clearing obstacles from your path. The blockage may be your own attitude to a thing or a person, ancient family karma, a person in the office or anything that you have at a soul level agreed to clear. Think of it as a log across your path that you have to step over, walk round, climb over or remove.

Grounding Portals

The earth dragons do not just ground people. If you build a dragon- or an angel-grounding portal, they will help to anchor and ground it into Mother Earth, so that it can remain in place as long as it is activated.

Place a ring of stones, pebbles or crystals in your home, garden, office or out in nature and dedicate it as a portal for the light. Then, call in the angels to bless it and the earth dragons to ground it. Activate it with prayer and an intention or by touching each of the stones or crystals with your finger or a crystal wand. You may be surprised to see or sense the angels using the ring as a gateway to step easily into Earth. You can make a fairy ring using the same method.

A portal is such a simple thing to create and yet can make such a powerful difference to a space. Also, it does not have to be set out for public view. You can place a small one in a drawer or a cupboard and it will be just as effective.

Planetary Service Work

The third-dimensional ley-line system of our planet, which has been our spiritual communication network for the past 10,000 years is in a woeful state of neglect and disrepair. The lines, like telephone lines, are blocked or broken, so that pure spiritual connection has become distorted or impossible.

Where lines cross or there is a major intersection of several lines, they have sometimes become tangled or cut. As planetary service work, you can send thousands of earth dragons through the network to clear, untangle, repair and cleanse the entire grid. If you then picture it glowing and working perfectly, this will enable the dragons to fulfil your vision.

The fifth-dimensional ley-line system is currently being reconstructed. It was active in the Golden Era of Atlantis. Now the dragons are taking it out of mothballs and polishing it up, clearing and repairing it as necessary. This is the crystalline grid that needs to be in place for the New Golden Age. It is a much higher frequency than the one we have been used to and again you can send armies of dragons to make it shine and re-activate it.

A new seventh-dimensional grid is now being created to allow the planet to take its rightful place in the universe as soon as the consciousness here is ready. You can help the dragons and Illumined Masters to build this, too.

Visualization to Remove Obstacles in Your Life

1. Find a place where you can be quiet and undisturbed.
2. Light a candle, if possible, to raise the vibration.
3. Close your eyes and relax.
4. Invoke an earth dragon and sense or see it plodding towards you.
5. Reach out and touch it and sense how solid and grounded it is.

6. Visualize yourself sitting on its back as you move together along a path.
7. You are aware of a log across the path. You realize it represents an unresolved problem in your life.
8. You touch the log. Then the earth dragon removes it.
9. As you continue to travel together you know that the dragon has cleared something from your unconscious mind.
10. You ask the dragon to transmute any negativity under your home or your office.
11. You both plunge into the earth and the dragon burns up any lower energies with its transmuting fire.
12. Invoke hundreds of earth dragons and ask them to unblock the ley lines of the planet.
13. Imagine them pouring through the ley lines and clearing them.
14. Thank them all.
15. Dismount from your earth dragon and open your eyes.

Chapter 3

Air Dragons

Air dragons are blue, the colour of the sky on a glorious clear summer's day and they bring inspiration, hope and lightness. When an air dragon approaches you, it raises your spirits in the same way as when you go for a walk in nature on a windy day.

This is partly because they blow the cobwebs out of your mind. These are the old, clogged, stuck thought patterns and ideas that humans tend to hold onto. Without us realizing it, they clutter up our brains with grey etheric stuff.

So, the beautiful air dragons waft away the old, unhelpful matter and then blow in new and better thought patterns. When they do so they bring hope and inspire fresh ideas. They stir wonderful creativity and higher visions. Often, when we are out in the wind, we think that we have let our own ideas emerge. In fact, we have created the opportunity for the air dragons or the angels to drop new concepts into our mind.

Because they can raise your consciousness, the air dragons enable you to see your life, your patterns and situations from a higher perspective. If you are feeling unjustly treated, bored or depressed, they can help you to rise above your earthly considerations. They can inspire you to take life lightly.

Air dragons can blow a vortex of cleansing energy through your home, your office, public places and situations if you ask them to, and replace the light there with a higher frequency. You may even feel the air moving. There will be a shift in energy.

Improving Communication

Air is the element of communication. These dragons use their power to enable you to speak honestly and to make people feel good. Ask them to inspire you to say the right thing and watch your relationships transform. Of course – you have to listen.

Bringing Inspiration and New Visions

Ask the air dragons to puff inspirational thoughts into the minds of teachers; integrity into decision makers; bright ideas into inventors; or to breathe higher dreams into people of influence.

The air dragons can make a huge difference because they carry in their energy fields the vision of the new golden energies for our planet as it could be. They can access the fifth-dimensional potential for us all. Like angels, they can light up our highest possibilities.

Joining in Fun

One of the many things I love about autumn is catching falling leaves. I often do this with my grandchildren. I even try to catch them when I am alone and no one is around. Then only my dogs look at me strangely! I make a wish when I catch one.

I used to ask the sylphs, who are the air elementals who fly with the wind, to help me catch the falling leaves. Now I invite them and the air dragons to join in the game. Not only is it fun but it helps to develop your relationship with them. When a falling leaf suddenly changes direction and lands in your hands, know that the dragons are enjoying themselves with you.

If you see the curtains suddenly moving, it may be the air dragons inviting you to play. If your candle starts to flicker unexpectedly an air dragon may be near, possibly drawing your attention to the arrival of an angel or to the presence of a loved one in spirit come to visit. If a little white feather dances in the air and then lands at your feet, an air dragon is doing the bidding of an angel by bringing a physical reminder to you that it is there.

Breathing Fire

Air dragons can breathe fire. So, if they are blowing away old stuff, they can make the clearance more powerful by puffing out etheric flames to transmute everything.

All beings connect to Source through the breath. The deeper our breath, the more air we inhale – in other words, the more Source energy we take in. When an air dragon is with you, it enables you to breathe more deeply. You are automatically more connected to Source. In fact, just thinking about an air dragon often triggers a deep-breath response.

Exercise to Breathe in Air Dragon Energy

1. Sit or lie comfortably and relax.
2. Let your breath become deeper and deeper.
3. Sense a beautiful shimmering blue air dragon flying closer to you.

4. Know that as you breathe in the air dragon is helping you to take in more Source energy.
5. Feel pure, white Source light bathing your cells.
6. Breathe the air dragon energy into your third eye, inspiring you.
7. Breathe the air dragon energy into your throat chakra, lighting up the truth of who you are.
8. Breathe the air dragon energy into your heart, filling your heart chakra with love.
9. Sense that at this moment your aura is sky-blue and pure, shimmering white.
10. Relax and feel the air dragon flying round you.

Visualization to Take the Next Step towards Your Dreams

1. Take a moment to decide what you want for the next step in your life. You may even choose to write it down as this helps to anchor your dream.
2. Light a candle and call in the air dragons.
3. Sit or lie comfortably and close your eyes as you relax.
4. Be aware of beautiful, warm, blue air dragons circling round the room puffing cleansing, purifying air into every corner.
5. Sense or feel them surrounding you, creating a vortex of energy round you.

6. Breathe this blue and white light into your heart centre.
7. An air dragon is inviting you to ride on its back. You climb on and feel totally safe and relaxed.
8. Together you are rising up and breaking through into a higher dimension.
9. From here you can see or sense the challenges you must meet to achieve your next step.
10. Your air dragon is inspiring you now, so that when it is appropriate you speak the most tactful, courageous or healing words.
11. You receive the energy to stand in your power with wisdom.
12. Your air dragon takes you to float over your dream as if you have already achieved it.
13. Take all the time you need to rest and relax here and absorb the assistance from your air dragon.
14. The air dragon brings you back to where you started and you thank it.

Chapter 4

Fire Dragons

The fiery red and orange dragons and the other fire elementals, the salamanders, can burn up and transmute lower energies. This allows the new to take their place at a higher frequency. Fire dragons are very effective as clearance experts, as fire is a most powerful element for purification and release.

From a human perspective forest fires or house fires are challenging or difficult events. However, they are often (but not always) directed by Spirit because it is time to let go of the old and bring in something better. Look at the way a woodland regenerates after a fire. Beautiful new growth arises from the old and covers everything in a mantle of spring green.

House fires literally transmute any negative vibrations that may have been held in that place for maybe hundreds of years. It is usually a major tragedy and loss for the person or people involved and takes them through an initiation into a higher frequency. Their soul has commanded this.

Salamanders are affected by human emotions and go out of control if people are panicking or angry. This can make a blaze much worse. However, fire dragons remain attuned to their mission and are totally disciplined in what they do. They add their fiery energy if that is required, or they withdraw if the conflagration is going as divinely intended. Our lower will and perception do not always see the higher plan.

Protecting Yourself with a Wall of Etheric Fire

Fire dragons are the master clearance experts and will direct their blazing flames at anything that you ask them to, transmuting lower vibrations that no longer serve.

If you ask they will create an etheric wall of fire round you, your home or your loved ones for protection and to clear energies that impact on you.

So, ask the fire dragons to burn up any lower vibrations round you. For example, if you are walking through a shopping mall, people will be emitting their frustrations and fears all over the place. If your aura is open because you are excited or even because you are exhausted, the fire dragons can place a wall of etheric fire round you, so that you do not take in other people's negative vibrations. They will also clear a path in front of you.

If you are on a crowded train or plane, or at any gathering of people, your aura will be bombarded by their vibrations. Remember to ask the fire dragons to burn it up and then place a firewall round you.

Clearing Your Soul Pathway

Fire dragons do not just transmute lower energies that impact on your life. They clear your soul pathway to accelerate your spiritual growth and will often burn up unnecessary challenges before you reach them.

Childhood and Past Lives

We are all the products of our past lives and of our childhood circumstances. Some of these strengthen or enhance us and your fire dragon can light these up to bring that energy forwards for you.

However, most of us have had experiences on our journey to the present that still hold a negative energy charge and impact on us without us even realizing it. For example, you may have had one or more past lives in which you have been executed, strangled or hanged. A residue of fear or pain from these may cause you to have throat problems in this lifetime. Call on the fire dragons to delve deep into your past lives and burn up those stuck energies.

We all have challenges and traumas in our childhood that create repeat patterns until resolved. Ask the fire dragons to help release them and inspire new and happier aspirations and patterns.

Family and Friends

You are not an island. When your family and friends are well and happy it is much easier for you to feel good. The fire dragons want you to feel happy so ask them to protect and inspire your loved ones, too.

Exercise to Transmute Your Patterns and Habits

1. Find a sheet of paper and some crayons.
2. Think of a pattern or habit you would like to release.
3. Write, draw or depict that pattern or habit.
4. Ask the fire dragons to help you to release it.

5. Burn the paper carefully in a fire or with a match.
6. Thank the fire dragons and resolve to be mindful of that habit or pattern.

Visualization to Burn up and Release Childhood Issues

1. Find a place where you can relax and be undisturbed.
2. Light a candle and dedicate it to your connection with the fire dragons.
3. Close your eyes and relax.
4. Invoke a fire dragon and see or sense it arriving in a blaze of orange fire.
5. Be aware of its sense of purpose and intensity as well as its impact on you.
6. Think of a difficult childhood memory or event that still affects you.
7. Ask the fire dragon to burn it up so that the energetic impact is released.
8. Picture the etheric flames clearing it totally.
9. Thank the fire dragon and relax, knowing you are regenerating yourself.

You may need to repeat this visualization many times, but each time it will make a difference.

Chapter 5

Water Dragons

Water elementals are a gentle green colour and smooth like snakes. They feel totally at home in lakes and oceans where they go with the flow. However, water is also in the atmosphere, so they are able to undulate and float everywhere with the cosmic current. Just think of one of these dragons and it will be gliding round you.

Unlike the dragons of the other elements, water dragons cannot breathe fire.

Keeping the Christ Light Flowing

Water dragons serve our planet by maintaining the constant movement of Christ light in the waters. With their enormous open hearts, they spread cosmic love wherever they go as they carry love in their essence.

The cells of our bodies contain water, so these dragons also keep the Christ light flowing through our bodies and those of animals. The more you relax and let go, the more easily they can touch your cells and light them up.

When you ask the water dragons to cleanse the cells of your body they will do so and this will enable you to be more luminous.

Let go and surrender so that they can access your energy fields to bathe you in Christ light. You will then radiate love and light and this will attract good things to you.

Christ light is protective and will shield you from lower energies around you. It is also healing and will raise the frequency within your body so that the old patterns or sicknesses can dissolve. All this will enable you to travel your ascension path more easily.

My Story

I was undergoing an initiation. This is a severe test during which all your spiritual guides and angels withdraw so that you experience your challenge alone. When it is over you have reached a higher frequency. I was seriously ill in hospital and as I lay there for several weeks, all my guides and angels disappeared. Only one small, green, water dragon sat by my bed. I knew that he was holding the Christ light for me and helping me to heal.

Circumnavigating Challenges

When you ask them to, water dragons help you to circumnavigate easily and lovingly round obstacles in your life. Every challenge is a rock in the river of your experiences. From the dragons' perspective they see the block and the way the energy streams round it, so they can find the easiest way to let the current help bypass it. In other words, they go with the flow. So many of us (me included) make our lives more difficult by launching ourselves straight at our tests when a circumspect approach would be much more profitable and tranquil. So, it is wise to listen to their guidance.

Promoting Harmonious Relationships

Water dragons also help you to offer tactful and gracious responses to people, so that relationships are harmonious and situations easier. Two of their great qualities are grace and harmony. They pour Christ light into relationship conflicts, smoothing different viewpoints and disagreements by pouring golden love and light into them. They can heal by washing away lower energies and replacing them with higher ones.

Developing Psychic Abilities

Water is the psychic element and these dragons help you to develop your psychic abilities. They do this by touching your third eye and allowing the chakra to open gently. For this it is important to relax, so ask them to help you rest and unwind by nudging you to flow with a smooth current. Some people do this naturally, but others find the guidance of the water dragons of inestimable assistance in de-stressing their lives. Your third eye only clears when you relax and raise your frequency. Then you can listen easily to your inner wisdom and tune in to your psychic impressions. Trust these dragons to help you do and say those things that will enable your life to flow smoothly.

Exercise to Bathe in Unconditional Love

1. Swim, bathe or shower.
2. Bless the water as you submerge yourself.
3. Call in the water dragons.
4. Ask them to fill the water with golden Christ light.

5. Imagine you are bathing in pure unconditional love.
6. Luxuriate in it for as long as you wish.
7. Come out of the water and thank the water dragons.

Visualization to Learn to Go with the Flow

1. Find a place where you can be quiet and relaxed.
2. Invoke the water dragons.
3. See or sense them undulating around you.
4. Notice that they leave a trail of glorious golden-white Christ light behind them.
5. Stroke one of the green water dragons and sense or feel how soft and smooth it is.
6. Ask it to help you flow round a challenge in your life.
7. Trust that it is helping you.
8. Ask thousands of water dragons to flow together through a place where the waters are polluted, dissolving lower energies and leaving a trail of the Christ light.
9. Thank these dragons and open your eyes.

Chapter 6

Earth-and-Air Dragons

The brown and blue earth-and-air dragons enable you to bring forward your visions and then ground them. They are excellent at encouraging you to energize all of your dreams and then bring them to fruition.

Their earth aspect grounds your vision, enables you to plan properly and make sure all the details are accurate. It is a solid, safe and commanding quality that causes those involved to trust and rely on you.

The air element inspires your vision with vitality and vigour, as well as the ability to communicate your hopes and aspirations with enthusiasm. This is the high-energy quality that attracts the right people and circumstances to support your intention. It provides you with all you need to take appropriate action.

The air and earth dragon is perfect to bring your life, as well as your hopes, into balance. Before you invoke this dragon, make sure your intentions are clear. Then ask it to help you to take the necessary action to manifest your vision into physical reality.

Help to Rise Above Your Challenges

In order to grow and develop on Earth we are presented with a series of tests and trials. The ascension path is not necessarily an easy one, though if we radiate enough light we will attract much assistance from the spiritual realms. It is very easy to get stuck in a situation or a relationship or to keep repeating a pattern because we do not learn the lesson and move on. It can be a great help if you can see it all from a higher perspective. The support offered by the air and earth dragons is invaluable as they enable you to rise above the challenge and at the same time stay grounded, so that you can find a sensible way to deal with it and go forward. They bring the balance that is needed.

Ask them to help you understand each lesson and the higher purpose behind it. This brings you a sense of accomplishment, harmony and satisfaction.

Visualization to Bring Your Chakras into Balance and Harmony

1. Find a place where you can be relaxed and undisturbed.
2. Invoke the air and earth dragons.
3. As one approaches you, sense its mixed energy and touch it with your hand.
4. Think of a problem you need to resolve.
5. Ask it to breathe rich brown balance and sky blue aspiration into each of the 12 Ascension Chakras: the Earth Star, base, sacral, navel, solar plexus, heart, throat, third eye, crown, causal, soul star and Stellar Gateway.
6. Glide graciously with the blue and brown dragon above the problem.
7. Relax as you do this and you will have a new sense of calm and equilibrium as you walk your divine path.
8. The dragon brings you gently back to Earth.
9. Thank it for helping you move forwards in harmony.

Chapter 7

Earth-and-Fire Dragons

These brown and orange dragons are extremely powerful for the earth element balances and controls the wild enthusiasm of the fire. While excitement and zeal are magnetic qualities that get plans started, they can let things go out of control or simply fizzle out. Too much earth thrown on the fire will put it out. When the earth and fire are in balance, inspirational visions can come to pass for it generates a contained energy. Earth-and-fire dragons are always in balance and can help immeasurably to move your business or family life or other plan forward, so tell them what you want to accomplish and ask them to help you.

Dragon Service

The earth-and-fire dragons are very much in service as they work with you to clear the ley lines of the planet. Because the dragons helped to build and maintain the original ley lines, they were known as dragon lines. These lines are now broken, tangled or distorted. The low-frequency light being carried is causing miscommunications. These ley lines are obsolete.

Currently a fifth-dimensional system is being laid to carry Christ light and love, so that the planet will be ready for the new Golden Age. The new network will only transmit communications that are at least fifth dimensional. It will be a spiritual network, sharing inspiration, beauty, peace, oneness and other high qualities, so that these can quickly spread.

The more we call on the dragons of earth and fire to move through the ley lines, the more quickly the fifth-dimensional grid will be completed, so that Earth will be surrounded by an interconnecting network of love.

You can also bring the Christ light down through your chakra system, then ask the earth-and-fire dragons to take the golden energy coming down through you and spread it in the ground where it is most needed.

Portals of Love

At the crossing points of the fifth-dimensional grid, portals of love and Christ light are being anchored. Ask the fire and earth dragons to illuminate and ground these. Then ask Jesus, the Bringer of Cosmic Love, to bless them.

Illuminate Your Challenges

Call on the earth-and-fire dragons to light up your challenges and tests before you reach them. This allows you to be subconsciously prepared to deal with them. These dragons may even dissolve them so that they disappear. Your life will become so much easier with the dragons' help, and you will be able to wear the golden Mantle of Mastery with power and assurance. This golden cloak is bestowed on you by Jesus when you take responsibility for your life and dedicate yourself to service with love.

Service Work to Illuminate the Fifth-dimensional Grid Round the Planet

Start by setting your intention to illuminate the grid of light round the planet. Now draw a circle to represent the world. Next, draw a grid over it with a yellow or a gold pen. You will see there are crossing points and mark these with a black dot with an orange flame. As you do this, focus on energizing the fifth-dimensional ley lines.

Visualization to Work with Challenges and Ley Lines

1. Find a place where you will be quiet and undisturbed.
2. Call a brown and orange earth-and-fire dragon to you.
3. As you stroke it, sense its balance and controlled passion.
4. Tell it of a challenge you face and ask for its help.
5. Know that the dragon will assist you.
6. Ask it to take you above the world to view the fifth-dimensional ley-line grid being built.
7. Now, ride on its back and look down at the criss-cross of golden lines.
8. Together you and the dragon serve the planet by visualizing a flame of golden Christ light at the crossing points.
9. See the whole world lit up and shining.
10. Feel the golden Mantle of Mastery, sparkling with stars falling over your shoulders, and wear it with integrity.
11. Thank the dragon when it brings you back to where you started.

Chapter 8

Earth-and-Water Dragons

These brown and green dragons are gentle and nurturing. The earth aspect offers a foundation in which the seeds of your potential can grow, while the water nourishes them so they can flourish. There is a season for all things in life and the earth-and-water dragons flow with the currents so that everything happens at the appropriate time for you.

Your seeds may produce a fresh idea, a vision, even a new awareness. Like any seeds they will need to be taken care of in order to fulfil your hopes. Ask the earth-and-water dragons to assist you in the perfect way so that you harvest great abundance.

Taking New Opportunities

These dragons will also help you when new opportunities present themselves. They will enable you to meet the right people and open doors that were previously closed, so that you make the most of the changes.

Preparing for a Fresh Start

It may be that you are offered a fresh start in some area of your life, maybe in business, in a relationship, a new home, travel or something different. The earth-and-water dragons provide the solid, nurturing, maternal energy, to enable you to feel safe and confident enough to go out and do it. They bless you so that it blossoms.

Having Fun while You Succeed

When you mix earth and water you create mud, which is a wonderful medium with which to play. So, this dragon brings you the energy to have fun. It suggests you do not take your new opportunity too seriously. Just trust it will succeed and enjoy the process. Remember that mud allows you to build constructively.

Providing a Solid Foundation

If you are planting a tree, you place it deeply in the soil to ensure that the roots create a solid foundation, before you water it well. In the same way, let the earth-and-water dragons help you to provide a good foundation for the next stage of your life.

Trusting Your Intuition and Acting on It

Water is the psychic, intuitive, creative element, so these qualities in this dragon will assure you that you know intuitively what to do and how to harness your creativity. The earth element will ground your action so that your plans blossom.

Exercise to Let Your Creativity Blossom

1. Find a sheet of paper and some crayons.
2. Decide what area of your life or what idea or project you want to nourish.
3. Call in the earth-and-water dragons and ask them to help you.
4. Draw the outline of a tree with deep roots under the soil.
5. Think about your vision blossoming.
6. Take a pink crayon and cover the branches with blossom.

Visualization to Help Manifest Your Project

1. Find a place where you will be quiet and undisturbed.
2. Call a brown and green earth-and-water dragon to you.
3. Close your eyes, reach out and feel its skin. Run your hands carefully over it.
4. Describe to it an idea, concept or plan that you wish to realize.
5. Ask the dragon if it will co-create this vision with you.
6. Picture your dream as if it has already materialized and place your picture into a bubble.
7. The earth-and-water dragon takes your picture and contracts it into a seed.
8. It places the seed in fertile soil and waters it.
9. When the seed is ready to sprout the dragon places it lovingly into your heart centre.
10. It gently breathes energy into it.
11. You both affirm that together you will bring this seed to fruition.
12. Thank the dragon and open your eyes.

Chapter 9

Air-and-Fire Dragons

This blue and orange dragon is about communicating your ideas with exhilaration and passion. The fire element is creative and enthusiastic and the blue aspect shares it with others in an inspiring way.

Expanding Your Creative Energies

When you open a window in a burning house, the element of air ignites a fireball, which may burn out of control. It can make a candle flame leap or cause a bonfire to explode. However, the elements within dragons are always in balance. An air-and-fire dragon fans the flames of creativity in a perfect way. It inspires the flames of your originality and imagination.

When you call one in expect your ideas to become great, your visions to expand beyond your wildest expectations.

The sparkling blue and orange dragons love to express themselves. If you are a singer, they puff excitement and passion over you; if a public speaker, they blow enthusiasm and charisma over you. They make you feel alive and able to speak out with energy and fervour.

This dragon does not have a grounding element, so it may create turbulence as it swirls around you. It can be unsettling or even overwhelming. This means it is important for you to be able to ground yourself.

Accelerating Your Spiritual Path

Fire is a powerful element for clearing your ascension path and transmuting any lower energies that have been holding you back. Harnessed with air, you communicate your visions with a vigour and passion that sweeps everyone along with you. Excitement and enthusiasm are very magnetic qualities, so calling in this dragon ensures that you race along like wildfire. Make sure you are earthed and sensible.

Serving with Passion

When you offer your creativity in service with light and joy for the highest good, an air-and-fire dragon is drawn to you. Decide what fires your enthusiasm and start to tell people about it. Your untapped resources will be brought forward, so harness your gifts and talents and trust the dragons to help you use them in the right way.

Following Your Dream

This dragon will inspire you to leap across the crevasse to hurry towards your dream. Don't stop to think. Trust your intuition and act on it. It is time for your soul to expand and grow.

Exercise to Take a Leap of Faith

1. Find a sheet of paper and some crayons.
2. Call your air-and-fire dragon and tell it you are ready to take a leap of faith.
3. Draw two mountain tops.
4. Draw yourself (a pin figure will do) leaping confidently from one mountain to the other, which is higher.
5. On the second mountain top draw an open golden gate.
6. Keep this image in your mind and watch out for signs from the universe.

Visualization to Stimulate Your Creativity

1. Find a place where you will be quiet and undisturbed.
2. Close your eyes and relax.
3. Call a blue and orange air-and-fire dragon to you.
4. Look into its eyes and feel the energy and passion it emanates.
5. Ask it to inspire and light up your creativity.
6. Watch as the air-and-fire dragon puffs a wonderful blue and orange flame over you.
7. As it flickers through you, it is gathering your creativity, talents and visions into a ball of fire.
8. It is shooting the ball of creative fire and expression towards your ascension path.
9. See your path of light becoming clear and beautiful.
10. See yourself striding majestically along it with creative fire pouring from your mouth as you express your enthusiasm and passion.
11. Picture the fire lighting up and inspiring people around you.
12. Know that the air-and-fire dragon will stay with you as long as you need it.
13. Thank it and open your eyes.

Chapter 10

Air-and-Water Dragons

These beautiful blue and green air-and-water dragons are light and flowing. When you add air to water it sparkles and bubbles, so if you ever want to feel vivacious and effervescent call in the air-and-water dragons. In fact, if you feel down or stuck, ask these ethereal beings to lift your spirits and inspire you.

Air inspires and water flows, so together they bring joy and ease into your life. These dragons fill you with bubbles of happiness and hope.

Connecting to Higher Frequencies

Because of their lightness and ability to go with the flow, the air-and-water dragons raise your vibration. They swirl round you, pouring Christ light into you and blowing you into higher dimensions. Because of this ability they help you to connect to lighter frequencies. They enable you to see from a higher perspective and perceive new ways of circumnavigating your problems. If you need to find a way to deal with a person or situation in your life, ask the air-and-water dragons to guide you.

Developing Your Psychic and Spiritual Gifts

The air-and-water dragons have a unique way of helping you develop your third eye chakra, which is also your psychic centre. Call on them to work with this chakra which, at the fifth-dimensional level, serves as a crystal ball. Know that this dragon will always work for your highest good.

Depending on what is needed within your third eye, the water aspect of the dragon may wash and cleanse the crystal lens and then the air will blow it dry. Or the air part will blow away any etheric dust, cobwebs or mist and then the water aspect will wash it. They will continue to cleanse your third eye at a rate you can cope with. This automatically hones your psychic talents, bringing you clarity and vision, so they encourage you to trust your intuition and other clair-abilities.

At the same time, these dragons will raise the frequency within this chakra to awaken and activate higher gifts, sacred powers and wisdom that may be latent here. They will then enable you to use your gifts for the highest good. They will also protect your third eye and, if necessary, call in other dragons and angels to ensure your true powers are safe and that no one can reach in and steal them.

Dissolving the Veils of Illusion

Across your third eye there are seven Veils of Illusion. The air-and-water dragons are really good at helping you to blow away the illusions before they wash the lens of your third eye. This enables you to see with clarity from a higher perspective and is the journey to enlightenment. You may have already totally or partially removed some of these veils.

The seventh veil is about half a metre in front of the third eye. It is red. When you recognize you are on your own individual soul journey and know that everything is love and light, the dragons can help you to dissolve this one.

The sixth veil is yellow. Believe in and trust the spirit world and use your third eye to transmit healing and higher thoughts. When you do this, the dragons can help you to dissolve it.

The fifth veil is pink. Love everyone in the world unconditionally. When you do this the dragons can help you to remove it.

The fourth veil is green. Honour and work with animals, nature and the elemental kingdom. Also use the power of your thoughts and visions to create and manifest correctly. When you do this, the dragons can help you to melt it away.

The third veil is light blue. Act as if you are an angel or an Illumined One. When you do this the dragons can help you to clear it.

The second veil is dark blue. Recognize oneness and accept divine abundance. When you do this the dragons can help you to disperse it.

The first final veil is transparent. Clarify your third eye and live in the seventh dimension. Then the dragons can help you to blow it away.

Attuning to Neptune

When your third eye chakra is fully fifth-dimensional, the air-and-water dragons will work with Archangel Raphael and his dragons to build and protect the link from it to Neptune. This is the planet of higher spirituality. Its ascended aspect is called Toutillay and when there is a pure channel of light between your third eye and Toutillay, you open to cosmic abundance as well as enlightened understandings about our world and the universe. You will see everything from an illumined perspective.

Expressing Your True Note

The glorious air-and-water dragons love to work with your throat chakra. They have the ability to enter this very sensitive centre to wash away old, stuck energy that prevents you speaking with clarity and truth. Then, they inspire you to express your essence.

This chakra holds blockages and trauma from those past lives when not speaking or acting according to the dictates of a paternalistic society meant dire consequences or death. Almost every soul incarnated in a female body has learned to conform in order to survive, as have many males. The same applies to children, who suppress their natural desires to try to please adults. It is time for truth and honesty to prevail, so that this chakra can shine out again.

Ask the air-and-water dragons to cleanse and free this chakra. When you know who you truly are and what you really want, your voice is attuned to your soul and you express a golden quality when you speak. It is time to express your real self and sing the true notes of your soul.

Visualization to Cleanse and Free Your Chakras

1. Find a place where you can be quiet and still.
2. Light a candle and dedicate it to your connection with the air-and-water dragons.
3. Invoke an air-and-water dragon to come to you and sense its blue-green energy around you.
4. Ask it to touch your third eye chakra (you may feel a fizzing sensation as the dragon works on it).

5. Request it to touch your throat chakra. (You may once again feel a fizzing sensation as old blockages are released.)
6. Let happiness and hope light up within you.
7. Ask the dragon to connect you with your inner song, so that you can express it.
8. Thank the air-and-water dragon and ask it to stay connected with you until you truly express your soul energy.

Exercise to Express Your Soul Energy

You may like to do this after the visualization. You may also like to do this where you cannot be overheard! Some people will find this easy, others excruciatingly difficult. There is no judgement, as we are all different.

1. Ask the air-and-water dragon to enter your energy fields and trust it has done so. Ask it to help you express your inner song.
2. Sing whatever note comes to you. Listen and feel the note. Is it melodious? How does it make you feel?
3. Try different notes and bring them into harmony. Focus on ones that make your body feel good.
4. You may find the notes sound and feel better in different places, such as by water, on a mountain, in the garden or in a particular room. Be aware of this and experiment until you feel happy with your sounds.

Chapter 11

Fire-and-Water Dragons

These colourful orange and green fire-and-water dragons are a very powerful force for movement and change. Together fire and water create steam. These dragons are very excited about propelling you forward on your ascension path. If you call one to you, relax and allow it to move your life on.

Powerful Deep Clean

Steam-cleaning is extremely thorough. Call in a fire-and-water dragon if you really wish to purify an aspect of your life. They can help clean out and remove old relationships from your consciousness or steam-clean any etheric dirt in your aura.

Preparing for Change

The fire-and-water dragons approach you when you are ready to make changes or a shift is being forced upon you. Call them to help you if you feel it is time for a new pathway or to deal with one of your challenges differently.

The fire aspect will help you in a number of ways. It will burn up the old that has been holding you back. It will fire you with enthusiasm for something or someone new and it will encourage you to make inspired decisions.

The water aspect gives you sensitivity, so that you use the energy correctly. It enables you to go with the flow.

Together they form the steam that gives you the power and energy to take action.

This dragon is always balanced, so the water cannot put out the fire, nor can the fire dry up the water! However, change does not always take place in the way you anticipate. So be prepared for the unexpected. Brace yourself for excitement. Look for transformation.

Being Ready to Light up Your Life

Have you ever felt bored, tired or stuck and then been propelled into action and excitement by an unexpected phone call? The fire-and-water dragons have the same impact as that phone call. You cannot be dull when they are on your radar.

If you are clear about the change that you want to make and are prepared for it, call the fire-and-water dragons and they will help you move forward as you direct them. When you are in control, they can be restrained in the way they power your journey up the spiritual mountain. You are the rails and they are the train and they will help you to steam forward and upward graciously.

Fun and Play

When this dragon is around it will lighten you up, for they love fun and play. You cannot be serious for long when it is influencing you. It will enable your inner child to laugh and be free. So, if you want to feel younger, think about the fire-and-water dragon and it will inspire and enthuse you to enjoy life. Be ready for more entertainment and excitement each day.

Exercise to Look through the Eyes of a Fire-and-Water Dragon

5. Imagine you are stepping into the body of a fire-and-water dragon.
6. Feel an inner glow as you raise your frequency.
7. Look at your world through its eyes and with its power and abilities.
8. Consider everything from a joyful perspective.
9. See the changes in front of you.
10. Prepare yourself for sudden change, knowing it will be for your highest good.

Visualization to Deep-cleanse Yourself

1. Find a place where you will be quiet and undisturbed.
2. Relax and close your eyes.
3. Call an orange and green fire-and-water dragon to you.
4. You may smile when you see the steam that is hissing from its mouth.
5. Ask it to send the etheric steam through you in a perfect way for a deep clean.
6. Relax and allow this to happen. Be open to anything that is being removed from your life.
7. Affirm that you are ready to expect the new and unexpected.
8. Ask the fire-and-water dragon to propel you into the new.
9. Breathe deeply and trust that the new is coming in a perfect way for you.
10. Thank the fire-and-water dragon and look forward to an enhanced future.

Chapter 12

Your Personal Dragon

Your personal dragon has been with you since your soul left your Monad or I AM Presence, which was your original Divine Spark. Your dragon was allocated to look after and protect you and to be your companion and guide. It works in a very similar way to your guardian angel, though they are on different wavelengths and are able to help you in different ways. It evolves and develops with you. So, the greatest gift you can offer to your companion dragon as well as your guardian angel is to develop spiritually.

Your personal dragon is usually the same element as your birth sign. At least it is predominantly of that element but may have one or two other elements if you need them.

Your Dragon's Love and Patience

Your dragon has enormous patience and has been waiting a long time to connect with you in this lifetime. It is also very wise and will always listen to you without judgement. It will try to guide you in a way that is supportive and for your highest good. Most of all it loves you from the depth of its huge, open heart.

How Your Dragon Can Help You

You can ask your dragon to stay close to you, so that it can race off to do something if it is needed. For example, if you are sitting in a café and a cloud of dark energy heads towards you, your dragon can charge over to it and consume it before the low frequency touches you and affects you. Or if you are swimming in the sea and a jellyfish is floating towards you, it can blow it away in another direction so that it does not sting you.

During your sleep it can fly with your spirit into other dimensions. For example, if you have a problem, it can take you to see things from a higher perspective. If you feel gloomy it can take you into happier dimensions to raise your spirits. If you feel disconnected from who you truly are, it can take you to your home planet (provided it is in this universe). If you pray to help others or to serve the world, it will take you where you are needed.

What Element Is Your Dragon?

If you are an earth sign – Virgo, Taurus or Capricorn – you will probably have an earth dragon.

If you are a water sign – Pisces, Scorpio or Cancer – you will probably have a water dragon.

If you are an air sign – Gemini, Libra or Aquarius – you will probably have an air dragon.

If you are a fire sign – Aries, Leo or Sagittarius – you will certainly have a fire dragon.

Your dragon usually has some of the energy that you most need. It invariably has the energy that is evident in your make-up. These may seem to be opposites, for example, you may need more drive so your dragon has some fire to try to push you forward; or you may have lots of drive, enthusiasm and ambition, so you certainly have a dragon with some fire urging you on.

Your companion dragon will probably have some earth element if you answer yes to the following:

- Do you love gardening, trees and plants?
- Are you very impractical?
- Do you need to be grounded, e.g. are you always thinking or dreaming?
- Do you stick at things you have started?
- Do you get too bogged down in things?

It probably has some fire element if you answer yes to the following:

- Do you pick up everyone's energies when you are in a crowd? (You need protective fire)
- Are you ambitious or competitive and determined to do well?
- Do you need more get-up-and-go or inspiration?
- Do you get fired with enthusiasm?
- Do you get burned out easily?

It probably has some air element if you answer yes to the following:

- Do you love being out in the wind?
- Do you need to communicate better?
- Are you inspirational and persuasive?
- Does your mind often feel clogged up?
- Do you need to be more light and playful?

It probably has some water element if you answer yes to the following.

- Do you love the water?
- Are you tactful and graciously persuasive?
- Are you too blunt and aggressive?
- Do you imagine challenges and obstacles that are not really there?
- Are you extremely psychic and intuitive?
- Is it hard to pin you down?

Visualization: Meet Your Personal Dragon

1. Find a place where you can be quiet and undisturbed.
2. Light a candle if possible, to raise the frequency.
3. Close your eyes and relax.
4. Invite your personal dragon to come to you.
5. Have a sense of its approach. Is it plodding or flying, floating or blazing towards you?
6. See, sense or intuit its colour or colours.
7. Feel the love as it sits beside you with its heart radiating towards you.
8. Touch or stroke it and sense how it feels.
9. Mentally thank it for coming and ask its name.
10. Take the first name that comes to you and honour your dragon by mentally repeating its name.
11. Your dragon has a message for you. Listen to it.
12. Your dragon invites you to sit on its back. You fly together happily with no purpose other than to bond and have fun together.
13. Your dragon returns you to where you started.
14. Thank it and open your eyes.

PART III

Fifth- to Seventh-dimensional Dragons

Introduction

The dragons in the fifth to seventh dimensions are helping humanity and the planet itself to prepare for the new Golden Age. Some of them cooperate with the Archangels and Illumined Ones to assist us in specific ways. Others bring the knowledge and wisdom of the stars and share it with us when we are ready. All are serving our world in incredible ways.

They all help us to transmute that which no longer serves our ascension path and to expand our light.

Chapter 1

Golden Christed Dragons

These beautiful dragons with huge golden energy fields are working very closely with humanity at the present time to touch us all with the Christ light. They are extraordinary in that they can access the golden Christ light at a ninth-dimensional frequency from Lakumay, the ascended aspect of Sirius where it is held in a golden globe. This is the highest level of the Christ energy that is available in this universe at the present time.

Golden Christed dragons take their fill of this awesome ninth-dimensional love and then can bring its frequency down to a level where it can be embodied by you. If you are able to accept a seventh-dimensional download of Christ light, they will pour it into you at that level. The vibration of this golden light cannot be lowered beyond the fifth dimension but more and more people are ready to take in this wondrous love energy at that frequency.

When Your Energy Is Higher

The dragons are watching your energy fields and the moment you raise your frequency, they pour more of the Christ love into you at the highest possible vibration you can absorb. Your frequency is higher at celebrations, when you are successful, when you are particularly happy about something, when you are in love or in a beauty spot in nature. At all these times they will be waiting to pour love into you.

Your Birthday

Your birthday is a special day! When you celebrate this day and give thanks for the opportunity to experience life on Earth, the golden Christed dragons and many other beings of light can get close to you. They will flood you with love.

Christmas

These dragons help the Christ light to pour into the planet during the sacred period between Christmas Eve and Boxing Day each year. It does not matter where you are on the planet or what your religion is, the Christ light touches everyone on that day.

I was so blessed in 2016 to be in hospital over the Christmas period. I was seriously ill and was awake most of Christmas Eve as nursing procedures were performed on me. I kept thinking that my illness must be happening for a reason as this was such a special night. And then in the early morning, a wonderful thing happened. The cleaner was banging the bed with his mop, which usually irritated me, but this time I was awed to see a torrent of deep golden light pour into the ward. It cascaded down through the cleaner and splashed and bounced like a golden waterfall full of rainbow lights until it filled the room and I could see it in my mind's eye spreading through the hospital and beyond. It was a moment beyond description and I shall always treasure it.

I knew the cleaner was a Muslim. At the time I was too ill to speak to him but, three weeks later when I was recovering, I asked him, 'If I mentioned the Christ light to you, would you know what I meant?' He shook his head. 'No,' he responded.

I smiled to myself because it does not matter what you believe or who you are – if your heart is pure enough, the golden Christed dragons use you to pour Christ light into the world.

Building Your Crystalline Body

When these dragons pour light into you, you are able to absorb it at a cellular level. This helps to build your crystalline light body for the new Golden Age when we will be expected to carry much higher frequencies of light. When you do everything you can to remain fifth dimensional and build your light body, it accelerates your ascension.

Ask the golden Christed dragons to pour their light into you for it will help you to remain fifth dimensional more of the time.

Carrying a high level of Christ light in your cells expands your heart. You can spread it out to the world. It also helps to protect you, for the love absorbs and transmutes lower energies around you.

Remember to call these dragons so that they can surround your aura with golden light and then flood your cells, too.

Dragon Companions

On several occasions recently I have been told by visiting friends that there was a huge golden Christed dragon sitting on my roof. On each occasion we were meeting to do spiritual work together. One friend told me that, when she set out to my house, a golden Christed dragon flew over her car all the way. She felt totally protected and also knew he was preparing her energetically for the work we were to do.

When your intentions are good these dragons accompany you and raise your frequency. You do not have to see them. In fact, they may choose to make themselves invisible. Just know that they are with you.

Golden Atlantis

Almost everyone who is on Earth now had a connection with Atlantis. This may have been in a physical body or as a spirit guide or helper. The reason for this is that we are tying up the loose ends and also bringing back the information, knowledge and wisdom of that time for use now. The golden Christed dragons, with their friends the golden Atlantean dragons, come to you to remind you of your special connection with the Golden Era of Atlantis. Ask them to awaken your memories as you sleep, so that you can access the wisdom held in your energy fields and your cells.

Visualization to Absorb Light from a Golden Christed Dragon

1. Find a place where you can be quiet and undisturbed.
2. Close your eyes and relax.
3. In your mind's eye, put down grounding roots and place a protection round yourself.
4. Imagine breathing golden love into your aura, so that you magnetically attract a golden Christed dragon.
5. Feel, sense or see the dragon alighting beside you and be aware of a great golden light surrounding you.
6. See the love and wisdom in its eyes.
7. It invites you to sit on its back and you are held in its deep golden aura.

8. It is floating gently up with you through the dimensions to see the ninth-dimensional golden globe of Christ light. Note how you feel as you observe it in the distance.
9. The golden Christed dragon is bringing you fully into the dimensional level where you can absorb the Christ light.
10. Rest here and breathe comfortably. You may experience golden Christ love and light flowing into you at a cellular level until your body feels as if it is sparkling and glowing.
11. The light from your body radiates out until the energy round you matches the golden aura of the golden Christed dragon.
12. Now the keys and codes of love in your energy fields explode like fireworks of love. You are building your crystalline light body.
13. The dragon returns you to where you started.
14. Thank it and sense how your energy has shifted. Remember that you can pass this energy to the people and animals you meet today.

Chapter 2

Lilac Fire Dragons

The lilac fire dragons carry the Lilac Fire of Source, which is a ninth-dimensional energy of transcendent love and enlightenment recently given to Earth. They can speed up or slow down its frequency, like being able to dim or brighten a light. They pour it into people and situations at the intensity required to offer transmutation and light.

This beautiful dragon breathes pure lilac fire over you, bathing you in love and divine feminine qualities. It enables you to release with calm and ease all that no longer serves. Then it raises your frequency to bring you peace, wisdom, enlightenment, joy and even bliss. It gently washes away any negative or redundant energy held in your heart chakra and when it envelops you in its lilac fire, it transmutes the old through the power of divine love.

Lilac is made up of violet and shining white light with a little pink of pure love added into the mix. Archangels Zadkiel, Gabriel and Chamuel all work lovingly with the lilac fire dragons. When you call on these dragons, the archangels are never very far away.

Divine Freedom

In the Golden Era of Atlantis, the Lilac Fire of Source, carried by the lilac fire dragons, was also known as the Flame of Freedom. It has the power to transmute, purify and cleanse gently yet thoroughly, then ignite with hope and inspiration. So, it brings true divine freedom. All chains and mental restrictions are dissolved. It frees people to live in their essence. The lilac fire dragons are now returning that gift of grace to us.

When you ask these dragons to come to you and envelop you in the Flame of Freedom, you can often sense the old restrictions falling away. Forgiveness flows naturally through you. You are filled with grace and tenderness. Ego issues dissolve. Then the dragons anchor the amazing light of the Lilac Fire of Source in your heart chakra.

Pure Ascension Tool

The Lilac Fire of Source is such a high-frequency ascension tool that you can only access it when you have reached a certain level of enlightenment and illumination. The lilac fire dragon can touch you with a diluted version of the Flame until you are prepared for its full power. In this way it raises your frequency gently. You can ask this dragon to stay near you and help you expand your light quickly until you are ready to fully anchor the magnificent Flame of Freedom. Then, it will take you into a glorious new and illumined way of living.

When this dragon remains close to you and swirls its lilac light round your energy fields, you undergo a rapid purification. From time to time you may sense your chakras becoming a column of beautiful lilac light. At others, your heart and throat chakras merge into a ball of blazing Lilac Fire. The people around you will sense and feel the purity of your essence and they will trust and honour you.

Helping the Planet

The lilac fire dragons have been waiting patiently in Hollow Earth, the seventh-dimensional centre of our planet, to come to our assistance. As more of us work with them, thousands of them are returning to the surface to help the world. It has such a huge ability to wash out entrenched negativity gently but deeply, and then transmute it, that we can call on it to clear the way for the planet to move through enlightenment and mastery into ascension.

Ask the dragons to ignite within you the Lilac Flame, and then tend and protect it. You can also request them to merge to create a massive ball of lilac light. Ask them to travel together over the surface of the planet, lighting up and clearing whatever is needed so that the ascension of Earth is joyously accelerated.

Ask these dragons to breathe their lilac fire into organizations, governments, corporations and all groups, so that heart-centred, honest and ethical living can once more take root in Earth.

Visualization to Illuminate the Planet with the Flame of Freedom

1. Find a place where you can be quiet and undisturbed.
2. Light a candle, if possible – a white, violet or pink one would be perfect.
3. Close your eyes and surrender to the lilac fire dragons gliding towards you.
4. Breathe in the purity of the love they radiate.
5. Sense the light spreading through your body, cleansing your organs and your cells.
6. Feel old cords and restrictions dissolving in pure love.
7. Feel or see the lilac fire illuminating you internally as well as externally.
8. Watch as the dragons anchor the Flame of Freedom in your heart so that you are entering a new and illumined way of being.
9. Send the energy out to illuminate everyone and everything around you.
10. Visualize thousands of lilac fire dragons lighting up places where they are needed.
11. See them hold the entire planet in the lilac fire of the Flame of Freedom.
12. Thank the dragons and open your eyes.

Chapter 3

Rainbow Dragons

A rainbow is not just a physical response to atmospheric conditions, it is also a cosmic portent bringing a gift from the universe to you. If your heart leaps with joy and wonder when you see a rainbow, you have accepted the gift. On the other hand, if you shrug and think it is simply a rainbow, you have declined the present offered to you.

When you respond with delight to the sight of a rainbow, the universe opens new doors for you. It may be a new job or relationship, an unexpected opportunity or an astonishing miracle. The universe works in many mysterious ways and often we do not recognize the cause and effect.

A Cosmic Gift

Like the rainbow arcing through the sky, the beautiful, mystical rainbow dragon brings you the gift of a promise. When you acknowledge it, a multicoloured, magical flame ignites within you. As you merge your unique energy with that of the dragon, it magnetically attracts something of special meaning to you from the universe. It may draw something from the universal pool of abundance or it may open doors of opportunity or re-ignite a beneficial past-life link that can be drawn into your life. When you connect with the rainbow dragons, magic is in the air. Look out for and expect miracles. Trust the universe to have your highest interest at heart.

At the same time, the rainbow dragon metaphorically takes you over the rainbow to find the pot of gold that awaits you. This mysterious reward may be the return of some of your own ancient wisdom that has been stored by your soul in a golden Orb in the planes of learning, which may have been waiting for many lifetimes to be accessed by you. Or it may be ancestral knowledge or wisdom that has been held in the Temples of Time within the Halls of Amenti, the learning halls in the inner planes. The rainbow dragons may even bring forward for you spiritual knowing from the vast storehouse of the collective consciousness. Do not be surprised if you have sudden insights or flashes of wisdom.

Sometimes the rainbow dragons breathe into your crown chakra and open one or more of its petals to access universal knowledge. They nudge you to use the knowledge wisely and for the highest good. They also remind you that when you share universal knowledge more will be downloaded to you. This keeps the flow going.

How Do You Know a Rainbow Dragon Is with You?

So, if you cannot see it or sense its presence how do you know this dragon has come to you? Of course, you may be presented with a physical rainbow across the sky. You may film a rainbow Orb or see a rainbow in a book or on television. You may catch a flash of multicoloured light refracted from a piece of glass. You may find yourself thinking of a rainbow dragon as it whispers to you of its closeness. These are your hints to expect the unexpected. Look for opportunities now. Trust and you will be rewarded.

Exercise to Work with the Rainbow Dragon

1. Find some coloured strands of wool, a range of coloured crayons, some multicoloured clothes and lay them out in a pleasing rainbow of colours.
2. As you do so, give yourself time to daydream.
3. Suspend the limitations of your beliefs.
4. Just float in a cloud of imaginings and maybe a rainbow dragon will draw close to open the gate of opportunity or wisdom.
5. Smile to yourself.

Visualization to Travel with the Rainbow Dragon

1. Find a place where you can be quiet and undisturbed.
2. Close your eyes and imagine a rainbow arcing across the sky.
3. See or sense a soft rainbow-coloured dragon emerging from it.
4. Watch it glide joyfully towards you.
5. Let your heart open with delight and anticipation.
6. As it stands in front of you its huge heart pours love over you and you stroke it.
7. It invites you to sit on its back.
8. Together you flow happily with the currents.
9. Suddenly a huge golden gate appears in front of you.
10. You touch it and push it open.
11. Your dragon says, 'Now look for the magic.'
12. And then it soars with you up the curve of the rainbow over the world and down the other side.
13. A pot of gold awaits you here.
14. Pick it up and hold it while the rainbow dragon takes you back to where you started.
15. Thank the dragon and open your eyes.

Chapter 4

Black Dragons

The black dragons are beautiful and very powerful. If one comes to you, rejoice because it is time for change and their arrival intimates you are ready for it.

The colour black symbolizes the Divine Feminine and this dragon carries all the qualities of love, caring, nurturing and compassion. It also holds the deepest mysteries and secrets of the universe. It brings magic to you.

Open Up to the New

When you are ready for something new to come into your life, these dragons hold you in a safe, dark cocoon so that the seeds of your secret hopes, your hidden talents and your divine potential can grow and develop. They encourage you to meditate or take time to reflect on your relationships or situation, so that the angelic realms can drop in new seeds, then nurture them and help them to germinate.

You may find that this is not just a small change in your life but that you are ready to undergo a metamorphosis. Perhaps your spiritual light needs to shine and radiate with new colours and at a higher frequency? It may be that your heart is ready to open in an entirely new way or that your psychic energies are about to develop. You may be preparing for a new job or parenthood or a move. The possibilities for transformation in your life are endless, so be open to the mystery and wonder awaiting.

If you have no idea what is emerging for you, relax. The seed may not have been planted yet. Then you go into the quiet and stillness so that the angelic realms can prepare the soil in which a new idea or concept can be planted.

You may see or sense a black dragon coming to you or you may be alerted to its presence by choosing that card from my *Dragon Oracle Cards*. If you sense a black shadow, do not be afraid. Just centre yourself and tune in.

A black dragon will make you feel safe and comfortable. When this dragon appears, you know it is time to rest and unwind, so it can help you to create magic and accelerate your spiritual growth.

Time to Relax

Black dragons also come to you to remind you how important it is to take time to relax and chill. If you go to sleep with your body and mind tense, you are not available for higher things. At the height of the Golden Era of Atlantis, the people could relax their bodies down to cellular level. This allowed the wise beings from other star systems, as well as the angels, to plant advanced concepts and extraordinary new ideas into their consciousness. It let illumined ones communicate directly with them. Are you ready for such knowledge? If so, the black dragons will be with you.

Soul-level Awakening

These dragons do not just help you to develop a new project or event in your life. It may be time for you to awaken at a soul level. If you sense this is the case, surrender to them and allow them to cocoon you so that you can undergo a metamorphosis. Prepare to rest, so that you can emerge like a butterfly and spread your wings. Expect life to be new and exciting.

Exercise to Develop New Potential

1. Collect together some paper and coloured pens or crayons.
2. Find a place where you can be undisturbed.
3. Quietly call the black dragons and trust they are with you.
4. Draw the outline of a big black cocoon.
5. In its centre draw a seed beginning to sprout green leaves.
6. If you wish, on subsequent days or when you feel it is the right time, draw more leaves.
7. Eventually, draw the leaves growing through the cocoon walls.
8. Know you are ready for expansion.

Visualization to Spread Your Wings and Fly

1. Find a place where you can be quiet and undisturbed.
2. Light a candle and mentally call the black dragons.
3. Relax as deeply as you can on each out-breath.
4. Imagine, sense or see these dragons placing their soft, silky black energy round you.
5. See yourself wrapped in their cocoon.
6. Relax into the safety and stillness.
7. Sense yourself curling up while magic takes place within you.
8. Let the black dragons soothe your mind.
9. Sense yourself expanding; be aware of your angelic wings growing.
10. Now, the cocoon is breaking and you emerge.
11. Spread your wings. Something has changed in your consciousness.
12. It is time to fly – soar like an angel.
13. When you are ready, return to land.
14. Thank the dragons and open your eyes.

Chapter 5

Silver Dragons

Silver is the colour of the Moon and is associated with the Divine Feminine. Silver dragons are incredibly wise and exude peace, calm and gentleness. When they approach you their soft silver light surrounds you and bathes you in a loving glow that melts away any deep pain that may block your soul progression.

With their silver energy shimmering in your aura you automatically touch others with this colour, so that they feel more balanced, calm and tranquil when you are near them. This soothing emanation allows people to treat you with loving kindness. It also attracts people with silver auras into your life.

Silver dragons inspire your mind with creativity, so call them to you if you want to express your originality, your imagination and your soul feelings.

See Your Divine Essence

The shining silver dragons come to you when your soul decrees it is time for you to recognize who you truly are. Many people acknowledge that they are made in the image of the Creator and that their essence is divine. However, it is one thing to understand this intellectually and another to know it, feel it and live it.

Silver dragons act as mirrors. When you look at them you can see your divine self reflected in their eyes. They show you your soul essence and remind you of your divine magnificence. You may even see for an instant the glory and beauty of the soul to which you belong. If their light raises you even higher, you just might catch a glimpse of your Monad or I AM Presence, the original divine spark of which you are a part and which appears to you as a glorious flame. It will illuminate you.

These dragons help you to see into your soul. This holds the keys and codes of the gifts, talents and wisdom that you have earned on your journey, as well as powers that may be locked away. They remind you it is time to look into your untapped resources and bring them forward. Only your fear of misusing them or that you are not good enough or worthy of having them can prevent you from revealing your true self.

They draw to your consciousness aspects of your potential and your true core that you may never have suspected you had. As soon as you accept something, they ignite it with pure white-silver light, so that you can start to express it. They enable you to get in touch with higher possibilities for your life. The silver dragons invite you to be ready to shine.

Prosperity

The silver dragons automatically leave a trail of prosperity behind them. If one touches you, unexpected good fortune follows. It may be a windfall, a pay rise, selling something for a profit or a lucky break. If you are setting up a new business and the silver dragon appears trust that it will prosper. The heavens are smiling on you, so smile back and flow with the success you expect. Remember that the silver dragon carries a feminine energy, so the prosperity it heralds calls for trust, acceptance, cooperation, working with others, generosity of giving and open-hearted receiving.

Dreams

Silver dragons love to travel with you in your dreams and flights of imagination. They puff silver thoughts into you to lighten and expand your ideas or see your soul gifts. You can invite them into your dreams and ask them to help you see into your soul.

Exercise to Attract Prosperity

1. Find a silver coin.
2. Breathe onto it and call the silver dragons.
3. Now hold the coin in your hands.
4. Ask the silver dragons to make your idea or business prosper.
5. Thank the dragons and place the coin under your pillow while you sleep.
6. Take out the coin and re-energize it each night for 30 nights.
7. Replace the coin under your pillow each night.
8. Expect prosperity.

Visualization to Look into Your Soul Mirror

1. Find a place where you can be quiet and undisturbed.
2. Light a candle and dedicate it to bringing forward your soul essence.
3. Close your eyes and breathe deeply.
4. Invite a silver dragon to come to you.
5. Be aware of a silver streak approaching.
6. You are surrounded by a cloud of silver. Relax into it.
7. The dragon is holding up a soul mirror and you look into it.
8. You may or may not see anything, but some of your soul energy is coming forward.
9. Know that your hidden gifts, talents or qualities may start to reveal themselves.
10. Thank the silver dragon and open your eyes.

Chapter 6

Orange Dragons

The desire to belong is one of the most fundamental needs of all people. We chose our families, our communities and countries before birth and this is usually where we feel comfortable and accepted.

Since the industrial revolution there has been a fragmentation of families. Wars have separated people from their loved ones. Mass migration has meant people find themselves on foreign shores. As a result, many people have wandered through life feeling alienated and disconnected.

Some people have awoken spiritually, so they look for the common humanity among people and seek to take down the barriers. However, a large proportion of the planet is still asleep.

Oneness will eventually be experienced everywhere. The feeling of belonging, the warmth and love of community is a start. The orange dragons are devoting themselves to bringing together soul families and soul communities in time for the new Golden Age. They light individuals and groups up so that they recognize each other.

These dragons breathe out flames of acceptance, warmth and happiness that connect people in peace.

Creating an Open-door World

In the fifth-dimensional communities of the not-so-distant future, people will cooperate with each other for the highest good. As abundance consciousness spreads, everyone will share openly as they did in the Golden Era of Atlantis, for they will trust in the support of the universe. The orange dragons are already breathing harmony and oneness over people. Many are absorbing this energy but, where they are not, the light will linger around them until they are ready to receive it. The dragons are now endeavouring to bring about a jump shift in human consciousness that will allow open hearts and minds to prevail. Eventually the doors of every home will be open to all whatever their colour, race and religion.

Awakening the Navel Chakras

Currently the fifth-dimensional navel chakras of humanity are anchoring and waking up again. This warm and welcoming orange chakra is located above the sacral chakra. When it is open we feel inclusive, interconnected and happy. The navel is linked to the Sun and the orange dragons help to bring down the keys and codes of Helios into this chakra. When all are connected we will at last be able to create a unified world.

The orange dragons are watching our planet to see where navel chakras are open and shining. When they see your orange light they know you are ready to spread the message of oneness and joy. Then you can work with the orange dragons to be a peace ambassador.

These dragons are often found round borders and boundaries, puffing their energy of acceptance and freedom.

Higher Manifestation

In the Golden Era of Atlantis everyone's navel chakra spun fast and radiated beautiful, bright orange light. Orange is the colour of creation and it was a very powerful chakra that the people of that time used for manifestation. In their navel chakra they would make a picture of what they intended to create, always for the highest good of all. The orange dragons would energize it and help take the picture up to the Soul Star chakra, where it would radiate out at a very high frequency. This allowed the universal forces to manifest it very quickly.

You can ask the orange dragons to pour their light into your navel chakra to enable you to develop your higher manifestation abilities. This confers power and must be used with care and discretion.

You can hold a pure vision for the new Golden Age to accelerate the ascension of the planet. This service work will be noted in your favour by the Lords of Karma.

Creating Community

The greatest work you can do with the orange dragons is to build community and togetherness. It may be to form an on-line community or to bring friends or neighbours together. Or you may be inspired to build bridges between cultures, countries, towns or schools. Ask the orange dragons to work with and through you. They will help you find the common humanity in situations, to see the divine in all people, to knock down walls of separation wherever they may be and to rejoice in the diversity of peoples, races and cultures.

Working with the Archangels

Archangel Gabriel is in charge of the development of the navel chakra and so the orange dragons automatically cooperate with him to build fifth-dimensional communities and bring families together with love.

They also collaborate with Archangel Metatron who works on a golden orange ray and is in charge of the ascension of the planet. They work through your light when you take action to help people of the world unite in harmony, or when you visualize them coming together. Archangel Metatron takes your intention and uses it to energize the plan for Earth. You are helping them to bring about higher peace.

Exercise to Help Build Community

1. Walk past your local village hall, church, sports centre or any community building.
2. Call in the orange dragons and mentally ask them to breathe their togetherness and peace into it.
3. As you breathe in, picture people being drawn together there in joy and harmony.
4. Thank the dragons for their help.

Visualization to Spread Peace and Friendship

1. Find a place where you can be quiet and undisturbed.
2. Light a candle, if possible, and dedicate it to higher peace and oneness on Earth.
3. Call in the orange dragons and ask them to blow into your navel chakra.
4. Relax and experience your navel lighting up.
5. All over the world (forget about the weather) see front doors wide open.
6. See people everywhere relaxed, at peace, communicating and smiling.
7. Visualize the orange dragons dissolving all boundaries between countries, religions, communities and individuals.
8. See Archangel Metatron taking your intention and adding it to the Plan for Earth.
9. Thank the orange dragons.

Chapter 7

Green Dragons

The green dragons look after nature. They passionately love the natural world, so they understand and protect its secrets. They will only allow these to be revealed to you when you are ready. For this you have to be in tune with the rhythm and flow of the seasons and the growth cycle.

Healing in Nature

Every plant, flower and tree carries its own individual divine blueprint and is linked to the collective plan for the species. Humans are totally dependent on the green world, so the Spiritual Hierarchy naturally expected that we would act responsibly towards it!

Every single thing that we need for our health and wellbeing is found in the green world. Originally plants were designed to rebalance any part of the body or organ that was slightly out of synch, in order to return our whole organism back to ideal health. This worked perfectly in the Golden Era of Atlantis, but once our karmic balance sheets started to get into debt we could no longer fully rely on plant medicine to heal us. This is when allopathic medicine gained its power. Now that karma is being rebalanced again, herbal healers are coming forward to help us and the green dragons are also returning to remind us of the gentle healing powers of the green world.

The healing property of nature is not just about the medicinal qualities of plants, though there is much more still to be revealed. Trees and plants hold wisdom and knowledge that will enable us to live in peace and harmony in the new Golden Age. The ancients understood the influence of the Moon, blessed water and certain crystals on planting and growth. They worked with the elementals, as well as the elements and the great energies of the universe, to bring forward abundant crops. The dragons are patiently waiting for our consciousness to expand to a level where we can accept it. As you care for the green world, these dragons will look after you.

Finding Answers

All answers lie within nature, and the luminous green dragons help you to find them. Ask them and they will direct you to the answer.

Sacred Geometry

Sacred geometry lies within the trunks of trees, pine cones, shells of snails, the pattern of a flower, leaves, everywhere. The Fibonacci numbers (a series in which the next number is found by adding up the two numbers preceding it) appear throughout nature.

When you are ready, these dragons touch your psychic chakras and help you tune in to and understand the keys and codes in nature, which bring you into tune with your divine essence. This is how the green dragons assist you to align fully to your soul blueprint.

Green Guidance

The green dragons are so attuned to you that they can guide you on your pathway, or to find the right direction or make the best decision. When you really get to know one of them, it becomes your friend and guide, helping you to connect and work with it.

Exercise to Ask the Green Dragons for Answers

1. Sit somewhere quiet and clear your mind.
2. Think of a question.
3. Call on the green dragons and ask them to help you find the answer.
4. Go for a walk in nature and relax and enjoy your surroundings.
5. See what the dragons draw your attention to, in order to answer your question.
6. Thank the dragons.

Visualization to Connect with the Green Dragons

1. Find a place where you can be quiet and undisturbed.
2. If you can sit outside in nature that would be perfect.
3. Close your eyes, call on a green dragon and sense it close to you.
4. Take time to stroke it, feel its skin, see its colour and have a sense of its qualities.
5. Ask it for guidance about anything you need help with.
6. Your gentle dragon takes you for a flight over the natural world. Together you drift through trees, over fields, rivers and mountains.
7. Let yourself relax and allow the wisdom to come to you consciously or unconsciously.
8. See it bring you back to where you started, and thank it for any revelations you have received.

Chapter 8

Royal-blue and Gold Dragons

Royal blue is a colour frequency earned over lifetimes on Earth or in other planes of the universes. It indicates that at some time you have practised illumined truth, honour and dignity. You have borne yourself with majesty and fortitude through challenging times. Royal blue also contains pure red, showing that you can take quick and appropriate action when called for, with a hint of the yellow of accumulated knowledge. Gold is the colour of wisdom. The magnificent royal-blue and gold dragons carry all these qualities. They truly are mighty etheric beings of light.

If you are connected to one of these gracious dragons – in other words you are reading about them, find yourself contemplating them or one comes to you in a dream, meditation or psychically – you have blue and gold in your aura or are preparing to gain those colours. These dragons are visiting you to prompt you that it is time for you to stand in your power with wisdom. You must bring true power and perfect wisdom into exact balance. So, call on them to strengthen you for this.

You can ask these dragons to take you into a past life or cosmic experience where you have attained these colours. For many people this was in the Golden Era of Atlantis. You may have been incarnated or have been there in spirit, working from the other side to support the vast experiment.

There have also been other times of opportunity when people have stepped forward with power and majesty. Letting these dragons show you your illumined achievement will help you to access once more the qualities that have been earned by your soul. Your memory may be activated consciously or unconsciously and then it will light up royal-blue and gold in your aura. This will bring forward the Cloak of Power with Wisdom you earned at that time, so that you can wear it once more with dignity and pride.

The Cloak of Power with Wisdom is bestowed on you by the mighty Archangel Michael himself. It is royal blue with a shining gold lining. It is different from the deep blue Cloak of Protection, which is the protective energy you can ask Archangel Michael to place around you. The Cloak of Power with Wisdom also has protective powers and has to be earned, so once you have received it, the first Cloak dissolves.

When Archangel Michael places the royal-blue and gold cloak round your energy fields, he also presents you with his Sword of Truth, which your dragon looks after for you. It will protect it and hold it in readiness for you. This is an etheric sword of light. You can use it in a number of ways.

When you are standing up for your truth, for what is right for you, against other people, you need the Sword of Truth. This may be about defending your spiritual beliefs when others are dogmatically opposed to you. Or you may need the power to tell your family what you intend to do when they do not approve.

If you wish to bring forward a knowing about something but the collective consciousness holds beliefs at a lower level, your soul intention is to pierce the Veil of Illusion. You will need the Sword of Truth to help you do this.

Those who explained that the world was round at the time the powers-that-be insisted it was flat certainly needed it! If you are bringing back wisdom about natural medicines, crystals, spirituality or angel messages, or you see spirit when no one else does, this dragon will be with you. Whistle blowers who reveal the truth even though it jeopardizes their career and journalists who dare to expose what is really happening are all supported by these dragons.

Your royal-blue and gold dragon carries the Sword of Truth for you and is by your side, ready to give it to you the instant you need it.

The royal-blue and gold dragons are very powerful. Once they become your protector, they will roar at anyone who tries to harm you physically or emotionally. Others may not be able to hear this but they will definitely feel the vibration. If someone assists and empowers your mission, they will support them too.

These dragons remind you that it is time to wake up to who you truly are. With their assistance you can stand with integrity in your power and majesty.

Visualization to Receive your Cloak of Power with Wisdom and the Sword of Truth

1. Find a place where you can be quiet and undisturbed.
2. Light a candle and dedicate it to connecting with the royal-blue and gold dragons.
3. Close your eyes and relax.
4. Invoke a royal-blue and gold dragon and see or sense it arriving.

5. Sit on its back and ride gently with it through the dimensions to Archangel Michael's sapphire temple above Lake Louise, Banff.
6. The temple's gold and sapphire gates fly open as you approach.
7. Archangel Michael himself awaits you in the Great Hall.
8. You slide off your dragon and stand in front of the Archangel.
9. He examines you carefully but kindly. Then nods.
10. Instantly a royal-blue and gold Cloak of Power with Wisdom is round your shoulders and a blazing Sword of Truth in your hands.
11. Feel yourself standing in your power with truth and honour.
12. Archangel Michael smiles and vanishes.
13. You return to where you started with your royal-blue and gold dragon.
14. You wear the cloak and the wise protector dragon holds the Sword of Truth for you and stays close.
15. Open your eyes ready to reveal your magnificence wisely.

Chapter 9

Rose Pink Dragons

When the rose pink dragons approach you, you are ready for the warm-hearted, higher love that they radiate. A pink rose is the flower of Mary, Queen of Angels, and spreader of love. And the colour rose pink is pure, soft and beautiful. Rose pink dragons are heart-centred spreaders of love, who cooperate with Archangel Chamuel to open and raise the frequency of your heart centre.

Your heart chakra contains 33 chambers that reflect Christ love. Each of the chambers of your heart contains a lesson that you have to learn before it can open fully. The rose pink dragons assist you to learn these lessons. The first 10 rooms are where we experience, overcome and transmute emotions. It is very easy to sweep uncomfortable feelings to the back of the heart where they block the doors. When that happens we keep the doors closed – or at least not fully open – and this causes us to withhold love.

It is often easier to open and cleanse totally the petals of the higher heart. The rose pink dragon with Archangel Chamuel holds the vision for us, that every chamber of our heart chakra is open wide and radiating love and light. Imagine a closely set spiral of 33 light bulbs. The outer ones are green, the next are pink and they are followed by violet-pink ones. The central bulbs are pure white. Each can shine 150 watts but some only look like 60 watts because they are covered in etheric dirt.

So the 10 chambers we humans have most difficulty with as we awaken to our spiritual journey concern being self-centred, fearing lack and a belief in not being lovable, rather than being joyful, living and giving. It is time now to clear them.

When you are ready to awaken your heart chakra fully, start by setting the intention to do so. Be prepared to forgive everyone who has hurt you as well as to forgive and truly love yourself. Develop the qualities of higher love such as empathy and compassion. Love animals, children, your friends and family; make your thoughts about others kind. Understand and be welcoming. Good thoughts make a good heart.

The pure white chambers in the centre of the heart chakra are about connecting with transcendent love, the cosmic heart, cosmic love and oneness.

The rose pink dragons can help you on your journey to fully open your heart centre. Think of any lower emotion you are holding onto and affirm you are ready to let go of your ego so that you can release the feeling. Then ask the rose pink dragon to consume the old stuff and dissolve it in transcendent love. Each time you do this you are allowing your heart to open a little more. Follow this by acting as if your heart is fully open. You can ask the dragons to build a portal or gateway from your own heart to the cosmic heart, so that you can immerse yourself in the love of the universe.

Romantic Love

Call on these beautiful dragons to help you if you are looking for romantic love. They will help to bring two people together who are on the same quest for romance. They see when two people have matching vibrations and work with their guardian angels to coordinate a meeting. They even assist lovers to bring their heart frequencies into synch to allow their relationship to flow more happily.

Transcendent Love

These pink dragons will puff their special pink transcendent love into your sacral chakra to help it to expand. This enables all your relationships to be more harmonious and your family connections to be more loving. Call the rose pink dragons if you want more love and warm friendships in your life.

Planetary Service Work

As an act of service you can also ask the rose pink dragons to sweep across the world, touching and opening hearts, with warmth and generosity.

Exercise to Open Your Heart Centre

1. Take a piece of white paper and some green, pink and mauve crayons.
2. Draw a spiral. On it draw 33 small circles to represent the chambers of your heart. Alternatively, you can draw a flower like a daisy with 33 petals.
3. Colour the outside 10 circles or petals green, then the next 10 pink, the next nine mauve and leave the innermost four white.

4. As you are colouring in the circles or petals, affirm that you are ready to release and forgive.
5. When you have finished, ask the dragons to fill the circles or petals with rose pink love.

Visualization to Fill Your Heart with Light and Love

1. Find a place where you can be quiet and undisturbed.
2. Set your firm intention to let go of your ego, forgive everyone including yourself, and open your heart.
3. Ask the rose pink dragons to come to you.
4. Be aware of beautiful rose pink dragons gliding round you pouring love from their hearts into yours.
5. Open the doors to the first 10 chambers and ask the rose pink dragons to enter and heal all that is inside them. See the old that no longer serves you being transmuted in pure love. See the radiant rose pink shining from each facet and filling your aura with pink.
6. Then move round the spiral and open the doors to the next 10 chambers. Repeat the above. See or sense each one light up and your aura becoming a brighter rose pink.
7. Do the same in the following nine chambers and watch or sense them light up and fill your aura.

8. As you open the doors to the four central chambers, pure white light pours out, and white diamond light sparkles in your energy fields.
9. Archangel Chamuel pours a shaft of rose-coloured light and love into your heart.
10. Ask the rose pink dragons to arc across the sky together, lighting up the collective heart of humanity with rose pink.
11. Thank the dragons and open your eyes.
12. Notice how you transcend your emotions as the rose pink dragons stay close to you and light you up.

Chapter 10

Golden Atlantean Dragons

Almost everyone on the planet had an incarnation during the Atlantean age because it lasted for 260,000 years, the longest civilization there has ever been. The golden era, when everyone lived in harmony and oneness, lasted for 1500 years of that period. People, animals and the land itself radiated golden auras. All the lightworkers here now were connected with that special time.

The frequency during the Golden Age was the highest ever attained on Earth. People had crystalline bodies, so that they could hold much more light than we can now. Light contains spiritual information, knowledge, love and wisdom. They were able to maintain this high frequency because they all had their fifth-dimensional chakras fully operational and so their 12 strands of DNA were connected and activated. Those living at the purest time of Atlantis had 12 strands of DNA fully connected. Within each strand of DNA were 64 codons or beads that enabled the people to live their extraordinary lives. The fifth-dimensional chakras were spiritual centres, holding the information that enabled the golden era to be so incredible, with its use of crystals, spiritual technology, mind control and cosmic travel that is currently beyond our comprehension. The Atlanteans' advanced spiritual technology was activated by crystals and mind control and is remembered as a myth or a dream in our subconscious. Yet the memory many still yearn for is the love and soul satisfaction that everyone then enjoyed.

The magnificent golden Atlantean dragons actively supported the energy at that time and they still carry the keys and codes of that awesome era. They approach you when you are ready to remember the wisdom of Golden Atlantis. The information for your Atlantean master body is held within your own personal fifth-dimensional blueprint. When you are ready to bring forward your memories and knowledge from Golden Atlantis, the Atlantean dragons will be with you to reactivate it and bring it to consciousness. This happens automatically as your 12 strands of DNA reconnect.

As Atlantis devolved, five chakras were withdrawn and these contained 44 of those codes. These disconnected codes contain our psychic and spiritual gifts, telepathy, telekinesis, powers of manifestation, clairvoyance, clairaudience, self-healing, regeneration and many other powers. Now that we are bringing back our 12 chakras, the golden Atlantean dragons are helping us to reconnect the codes to awaken our knowledge, gifts and talents. This will also lift the Veil of Amnesia and you can then truly recognize oneness and merge into it.

Reconnecting Your DNA

During the golden era the people learned to relax right down to a cellular level. This meant that the beads or codons within the DNA in the cells could loosen and lie side by side, so that they touched each other and were fully connected. So step one is to relax deeply.

Love is of the essence, so develop compassion, empathy and generosity. This raises your energy frequency. And joy, happiness, laughter, positive living, pure fun and enjoyment of life are important qualities for the reconnection of our DNA.

At full moons and other times, bursts of cosmic energy are now being downloaded by the Intergalactic Council to reactivate the transcendent chakras again. If you are ready, ask the golden Atlantean dragons to help you to take advantage of these opportunities and they will enable you to switch on your 12 strands of DNA again.

There is one other important condition and that is the atmosphere and energy around you. It needs to be high enough for the activation to take place, so surround yourself with high-frequency people and live in pure conditions.

The Great Crystal

The Great Crystal of Atlantis was housed in the Temple of Poseidon and was powered by pure Source energy. This was the generator of power for the entire experiment of this golden era. Although the Great Crystal fell into the ocean into the centre of the Bermuda Triangle when Atlantis collapsed, it continued to be an occasionally used portal and generator, protected by water dragons.

At that time the golden Atlantean dragons withdrew from Earth as their frequency was too high to connect with humanity. Now at last the Great Crystal has awoken again and has started to spout a fountain of golden light over the planet once more. The golden Atlantean dragons have been able to return to remind us of who we are and what we can accomplish. Not only are they repairing our foundation for the future, but they are preparing us to build again at a level higher.

The Masters of Atlantis

The High Priests and Priestesses were fifth- to sixth-dimensional and they oversaw the running of the planet. They were in direct communication with the Intergalactic Council and the Masters of many star systems. The golden Atlantean dragons worked with them, and supported and protected them. They often went with them through the dimensions when they were travelling out of body to consult wise ones elsewhere in the universe.

These dragons remember exactly who you were during that epoch, what you did, the quality of your light and your soul mission. They can breathe these memories into your third eye in a burst of golden fire to awaken you. As you stand in your golden Atlantean mastery once more, your Veils of Illusion will start to dissolve.

Like many dragons the golden Atlantean ones are clearance experts and can dissolve anything that no longer serves you from around that era that you are ready to release. Then the light can return. This dragon will stay with you as you prepare once more to be an Atlantean Master.

Visualization to Help Reconnect Your 12 Strands of DNA

1. Find a place where you can be quiet and undisturbed.
2. Light a candle and dedicate it to working with the golden Atlantean dragons.
3. Close your eyes and relax as deeply as you can.
4. Invoke a golden Atlantean dragon and see or sense it approach you in a flash of golden light.
5. Ask it to pour its golden fire into your heart to expand your possibilities and start to reconnect your 12 strands of DNA.
6. Imagine your strands of DNA are like two strands of beads lying side by side in the cells in your body, touching and relaxed.
7. Relax more and more as you are enveloped in golden fire.
8. Now ask it to pour golden fire into your third eye to awaken your memories.
9. Trust that a shift is happening.
10. Thank the dragon and open your eyes.

After you have completed the visualization, remember to stand tall as a radiant Atlantean Master with a golden aura.

Chapter 11

The Peach and Gold Peace Dragons

Many of the archangels have peace dragons working with them, on different colour frequencies. For example, Archangel Uriel's golden dragons spread peace with wisdom; Archangel Christiel's moon-white dragons spread peace with higher spiritual understanding. However, while writing this book I was approached by the peach and gold peace dragons who wanted to be included. They are incredibly beautiful and ethereal, as they shimmer and sparkle with their delicate colours. Peach includes the pink of love and gold of wisdom. The golden hue they radiate is a very pale high-frequency light. They influence others with love and wisdom to find peace. They were magnificent to see and feel.

Bringing Harmony

I was quite surprised to see a peach and gold peace dragon as its energy seemed more like that of an angel than a dragon, and it kept impressing visions of peace on me. I realized the dragon was telling me that it works with people by bringing them into harmony. It asked me to imagine I had been given the gift of peace. It blew energy through me to fill my body, mind and heart with peace – a wonderful sensation – and I immediately felt incredibly loved with a knowing that all is well. My aura became peach-gold and reached out around me.

Then it took me into my inner world to touch others with this energy. Wherever it led me, a finger of peach-gold would reach out from my aura to people and they would immediately become centred, still and in harmony. Their hearts would gradually fill with soft pink and open up. They would be at peace.

Touching Others with Peace

Several nights running, as I rode on its back, the peach and gold peace dragon took me to meeting places. The dragon's energy would flow through me and spread over the people like a drop of oil on troubled waters. Once we were in a place where there was dark corruption. My steed went directly up to one rather portly man and stood in front of him but the man could not see it. When my dragon turned and looked at me, I knew my task was to ask him to touch the person. No sooner had I done so than the dragon put its head right up to the man's chest and blew. The peach and gold light shot into his aura. He looked puzzled. Then his heart, which had been closed tight as a bud, started to expand. I don't know if he made different decisions after this, but I am sure that new possibilities had been opened up for him.

Living with the Peach and Gold Peace Dragon

When you ask the peach and gold peace dragon to live with you all the time, your life feels different. You can invite it into your aura, in which case you will sense the incredible gentle love, peace, harmlessness and grace that it emits all the time. You will feel calmer so that things that once mattered will not seem so important. You become more centred and patient, more gentle and loving, but you can still defend yourself if you need to. You can fight your corner and stand up for yourself yet you do not need to, because your energy has become accepting, enfolding, calming, soothing and enlightening. This means others feel safe with you, respect you and honour your light. Reaching this state does not happen overnight, but if you set this as your goal and intention, the peach and gold peace dragon can have a powerful impact on you.

Alternatively, or in addition, you can ask this dragon to blow its peace energy into your aura and into your 12 chakras. Sense or feel your spiritual centres spinning faster. Constantly talk to the dragon about living in peace and spreading it. Wherever you go imagine you are in a column of peach and gold light. Sense the fingers of peace moving out from you to enfold those around you.

Planetary Service Work

If you wish to send these peach and gold peace dragons to touch places, people and situations, first ask them to fill your being with their peace light, and breathe it in. Then ask them to pour their frequency of peace over individuals and assemblies of people, into situations and places. You can create a bridge of peach-gold light to places where people gather to make decisions, then command thousands of peach and gold dragons to go across it to spread peaceful thoughts. Their energy can open hearts and minds.

Helping Animals

You can also send the peach and gold peace dragons to businesses that farm animals intensively to try to raise the animals' frequency, for through peace comes oneness. This will help the animals that are treated as commodities to bear the slavery that is imposed on them.

Visualization to Spread Peace

1. Find a place where you can be quiet and undisturbed.
2. Light a candle and dedicate it to living in peace with love and wisdom.
3. Close your eyes and relax with centred, peaceful thoughts.
4. Call in the peach and gold peace dragons and you may feel a faint movement of air as they gently surround you.
5. Feel or sense them blowing peach and gold peace into your heart and feel it open and soften.
6. Be aware of your aura filling with peach and gold light, so that you become a peace flame.
7. One of the dragons invites you to sit on its back and together you create an ethereal, calm flame.
8. You fly together into your home or office. Here peach and gold peace spreads from you and fills the space. It touches and soothes the minds and hearts of all.
9. Next, you fly together to a place in the world where there is unrest. As you hover over the people, fingers of peach and gold flame reach out and touch the minds and hearts of all the angry people.

10. Sense or imagine them relaxing, becoming grounded and centred, and seeing things from a higher, peaceful, wise perspective.
11. Know that you are leaving behind the peace energy and that it will go to where it is most needed.
12. Return to where you started and thank your dragon.

When you work with this dragon at night, you become a peace ambassador and maybe even an intergalactic peace ambassador in the inner planes. You can be an immense force for good.

PART IV

Dragons That Work with Archangels and Masters

Introduction

Certain dragons work in cooperation with their archangels or masters, though they are on different wavelengths. While the archangel holds the vision, their dragons clear the lower energies that block the pure intention.

For example, if you ask Archangel Jophiel and his crystal yellow dragons to help you open the thousand petals of your crown chakra, they will liaise with each other to assist you for your highest good. Archangel Jophiel will raise the frequency of your crown chakra, so that the doors to the thousand chambers start to open. The crystal yellow dragons will help each petal within the chambers to grow and reach out to the stars. The dragon will untangle those that need to be freed. As a team they enable your crown chakra to operate fully much more efficiently than if one of them was working alone.

When you feel a rapport with one of these dragons it automatically helps you to attune with its complementary archangel or master.

Chapter 1

Archangel Zadkiel's Gold and Silver Violet Flame Dragons

Archangel Zadkiel is pure violet, the colour of deepest spiritual transmutation. In the era of Golden Atlantis everyone could access their Violet Flame to burn away any lower energies around them or any situation. This enabled the citizens to keep everything clear and pure at all times. The mighty St Germain, who is now Lord of Civilization, one of the highest positions in this universe, also carries the Violet Flame. When Atlantis degenerated, the Flame was withdrawn into the inner planes because its power could be misused.

Harmonic Convergence

In 1987, at a significant planetary alignment called the Harmonic Convergence, so many people prayed for help for the planet that St Germain took a petition to Source asking to bring back the Violet Flame. This was granted and some violet dragons returned to Earth.

The Cosmic Moment

In 2012, when the dragon portals opened, huge numbers of dragons came back, among them many violet dragons. The Silver Flame of Grace and the Gold Flame of Wisdom of Atlantis merged with the Violet Flame and became the Gold and Silver Violet Flame. The violet dragons absorbed the expanded higher-frequency flames and became the Gold and Silver Violet Flame dragons. This enables them to transmute lower energies with grace and wisdom and transform them into something much higher.

They will help you to transform yourself and everything around you graciously. Within this energy magical healing can take place.

Divine Alchemy

St Germain, who was Merlin in one of his lives, was the greatest alchemist our world has ever known and the Gold and Silver Violet Flame dragons carry his power. They, too, are divine alchemists. They link you into St Germain and Archangel Zadkiel whenever you connect with them. Not only are you engulfed in the violet flames that transmute the old and raise the frequency to a higher level than before, but the silver flames bathe you in the Divine Feminine, while the gold flames touch you with wisdom. At the same time St Germain and Archangel Zadkiel both illuminate you.

Release the Past

You can ask Archangel Zadkiel's Gold and Silver Violet Flame dragons to help you release the past. Think of a situation that still has an emotional impact on you and call in these dragons. Hold the intention of clearing that event or trauma completely from your energy fields and the cells of your body. To do this you must be prepared to forgive everyone concerned, including yourself, for what happened. The source of this may have been in a past life but this makes no difference. Your intention and the grace of these dragons is all important in order to consume the old. When you do invoke them they will light you up and engulf you in their magnificent transmuting gold, silver and violet flames.

Ask them to replace the old with new light and joyful beautiful energy. Like all spiritual work you may have to do this many times, but eventually it must set you free.

Golden Protection

The violet flame dragons open up your aura so that you need to protect your energy fields. The Gold and Silver Violet Flame dragons also open you up as they consume the lower energies within your field but, at the same time, the golden flame places a protection around your aura. You may like to ask them to add extra golden flames to ensure that you are totally shielded and safe.

Cleanse Your Aura

One of the easiest and most effective ways to cleanse and purify your aura is to call in the Gold and Silver Violet Flame dragons to burn up lower frequencies. They will fill you with high-vibration etheric fire. They will also burn up discordant energies that are coming towards you from others. And they raise your light. For a moment you yourself become a gold, silver and violet fire.

Service under Grace

The dragons have returned to serve the planet. Because of free will they need you to send them to people, places and situations to burn up conditions that have been holding us all back. You cannot influence anyone's karma or change their circumstances unless you have their permission or that of their higher self. If you do influence them and it turns out badly, you take on their karma. However, you can ask the Gold and Silver Violet Flame dragons to burn up the negativity of a situation around someone under grace. This means that it will only be done if their higher self agrees. This enables you to relax and offer your service, with the assurance that you are working with spiritual law.

Exercise to Help Cleanse and Heal under Grace

1. Find a place where you can be quiet and undisturbed.
2. Light a candle and invoke the Gold and Silver Violet Flame dragons.
3. See or sense them swirling round you awaiting your instructions.
4. Command them to go under grace to a person, place, situation, meeting place, country or somewhere important to burn up lower energies.
5. Picture the dragons racing to fulfil your command and pouring their etheric fire into it.
6. Feel, sense or see the flames engulfing and healing the person, place, situation, meeting place or country.
7. Picture the new and higher-frequency energy taking its place.
8. Be aware of St Germain and Archangel Zadkiel blessing the outcome.

Visualization to Transmute Low-frequency Energies

1. Find a place where you can be quiet and undisturbed.
2. Light a candle and dedicate it to your connection with the Gold and Silver Violet Flame dragons.
3. Decide on something that no longer serves you.
4. Close your eyes and relax.
5. Invoke the Gold and Silver Violet Flame dragons and feel their flames swirling round you.
6. Picture that which you wish to transmute being etherically dissolved in the violet, silver and gold flames.
7. Ask the dragons to replace it with new and joy-filled opportunities at a higher frequency.
8. Know that they are starting to work with you.
9. Thank them and open your eyes.

Chapter 2

Thor's Red, Black and Gold Dragons

Thor had many incarnations during which he mastered the element of fire. He could light it, make it blaze, move it, diminish it or extinguish it. He could command fire with the power of his mind to such a degree that he became the God of Thunder. The red, black and gold dragons work directly under the command of Thor, Elemental Master of Fire.

Archangel Gabriel

Archangel Gabriel is the angelic being in overall charge of fire and he directs Thor and his dragons. Archangel Gabriel sends these dragons to places or situations where they are needed. They use the power of fire to clear and transmute the old and to allow regeneration where it is needed.

Humans Affect the Elements

Fires do not happen by chance. Even wildfires start with a purpose. However, salamanders, who are fire elementals, are very influenced by human energies. When we become excited or afraid, they latch onto our energy and go wild. Then fires can run out of control and change the divine plan. We humans can hugely affect fires (or hurricanes, earthquakes or floods) by using our free will sensibly to send calm, peaceful thoughts to soothe the elementals.

Dragons are wise old beings who carry out their missions in a strong and steady way. They are not influenced by human emotions and thoughts. So, you can send them to challenging situations knowing they will hold steadily to their purpose.

Warning Signs

Thor's red, black and gold dragons are very powerful fire elementals. Red and black together are warning signs in nature that say, 'Do not mess with me!' – they suggest energy and ability to take action. Thor's dragons have also earned the colour gold, which indicates that they will use their power and energy with wisdom. They still radiate the message, 'Do not mess with me!' but demonstrate that any action will be tempered with sense.

Peaceful Warriors

These dragons are connected with the ascended part of the red, warrior planet Mars, called Nigellay. They act as spiritual, peaceful warriors throughout this universe. They patrol everywhere to make sure that all is as it should be. They help the weak and moderate the actions of the strong. Where there is disruption or disagreement they act as policemen and return things to equilibrium with the power of wise action. Then they can consume the dense energies that have been created.

Because we received the gift of free will, Earth has largely been left alone. We have not been ignored. Rather, the spiritual realms have been watching human activity on our planet with increasing concern. But now the whole world is poised to change and at last we are ready for Thor's red, black and gold dragons. They have arrived here to act as peaceful warriors but can only do so with our permission. The more often we ask them to patrol our world, breaking up conflict, helping the weak and dispossessed, disempowering bullies so that their victims can breathe freely, helping people to understand animals, the quicker the new will come about.

When a country or group of people is threatening another one or creating unfair conditions or terms, send in these dragons to break up the lower energy and bring in wisdom. If corporations or organizations are using unfair tactics, you can ask Thor's red, black and gold dragons to influence them to help employees, customers and, ultimately, everyone.

So, you can help the red, black and gold dragons and the world by sending them to places or situations that need their help. You can assign single warrior dragons or you can ask armies of them to do the light work. They will always do precisely what is right for everyone for the highest good. If a country, a corporation, a group or an individual collapses economically, or in any other way, the help of these dragons is exactly what is needed.

How the Red, Black and Gold Dragons Help You

You can ask them to help you change conditions or circumstances in your own life. It may be time to move on from a relationship and you want help to do it in a clean way. Perhaps you are being disempowered by a person or an organization. If so, you can ask these dragons to assist you to stand in your power again. They will clear the energies round you as you make this transformation for they are totally dedicated to helping you with love and wisdom.

If one of these dragons appears to assist you, you have earned the right to receive their support. This life is the culmination of many lives and it is time for you to be set free, so that you can progress. They will always protect you.

Visualization to Help You Move On in Your Life

1. Find a place where you can be quiet and undisturbed.
2. Light a candle and dedicate it to working with Thor's red, black and gold dragons.
3. Close your eyes, relax and invoke the dragons.
4. Sense or see them clearing the energy around you.
5. Tell them about any situation or relationship that you are ready to move on from. This could be changing family patterns, moving house or anything that is right for you.
6. Be aware of the dragons zooming around what you want to let go of.
7. As the old energy breaks up, see it filling with a trail of gold and know that the desired change is starting.
8. Now extend the desire for positive change to the planet by sending an army of dragons to break up the lower vibrations around dishonest or greedy corporations, organizations or countries.
9. See the dragons fanning out to do what they need to do.
10. See the situation surrounded with golden light.
11. Thank these dragons and know that they will continue to work with your request.

Chapter 3

Archangel Mariel's Magenta Dragons

Archangel Mariel is in charge of your Soul Star chakra and works with the magenta dragons. These dragons accompany you on your eternal soul journey and, when you are ready, they will nudge you to wake up to who you truly are. They also enable you to bring forward your soul wisdom and accelerate your ascension in this lifetime. Their ultimate aim is to help you merge with your higher self so you live your life in a totally different way.

Your Soul Journey

Your Monad or I AM Presence is the twelfth-dimensional part of you. This mighty flame beyond human comprehension is a fragment of Source light, sent out to experience creation and ultimately to return those experiences to the Godhead. Your Monad sent out 12 sons/daughters, or parts of itself deeper into matter to bring learning back home.

These sons/daughters are your higher self or soul, which again is a magnificent flame, though not as bright as your Monad.

When your soul becomes fully twelfth dimensional it starts to merge back into the Monad, though it may choose to remain separate to assist others.

Each soul in turn dispatched 12 sons/daughters into the universes to learn and bring their new knowledge back to the soul. This is the part of you that is experiencing life here. It is known as a soul extension or your personality self.

There are aspects of you, who are soul brothers, sisters and cousins, all on the same quest to expand their light and bring it home. You may have met them or they may not be on Earth at the same time as you are. They may be in another planet, universe, plane or dimension but you can still connect with them.

As soon as your 12 fifth-dimensional chakras are anchored and spinning fast, a magenta dragon will be with you, helping to awaken soul memories.

The Veil of Amnesia

When we travel through the universes, planes and dimensions, we always remember where we have come from and our origins. However, before we incarnate on Earth we go through the Veil of Amnesia and forget everything. This is because we have entered the plane of free will, which was set up here by Source and the Intergalactic Council as an experiment. The aim was to see if we could come to this dense physical space, look after a physical body and keep our connection to Source, while having free will to make our own decisions.

Only brave souls dared to accept the invitation to go on such an expedition into the unknown. But millions did volunteer. No one could forecast what would happen here. A system of karma was set up so that souls would recognize that there was a consequence to every freely made decision. Once you had signed on for this journey, you had to return again and again until you got it right.

This is one reason why there are seven billion individuals on the planet right now. The next step in the experiment starts in 2032 and everyone wants to clear their karma so that they can move on. Many of them were over-optimistic about their ability to handle earthly conditions and their own karma and this contributes to the turmoil everywhere.

And yet millions are waking up and the magenta dragons are here in force assisting them to prepare for the new Golden Age.

How the Magenta Dragons Help You

When a magenta dragon sees that your light is blazing, it approaches you and starts to build a huge, deep pink flame of love around you. This is filled with higher spiritual knowledge, understanding and wisdom. The magenta dragon uses this to prepare you to accept who you truly are. It starts to dissolve the Veil of Amnesia so that you can begin to remember your origins, your soul journey, your gifts, talents and wisdom. Then you become an Enlightened One.

The magenta dragons and Archangel Mariel's angels hold all the information about your entire journey through many planes and dimensions, on other stars and planets throughout the cosmos. They constantly remind you that you are really a great illumined being with a unique role in the universe. You have much to offer or you would not be reading about the magenta dragons! They are assisting you to access your higher self and ultimately merge with it, so that you see all with eyes of love and wisdom.

Your Magenta Soul Star Chakra

The soul star is the 11th spiritual wheel in the fifth-dimensional chakra column. It reflects Archangel Mariel's magnificent light and records the entire experience of your soul and that of your soul brothers and sisters. Your true, vast light can be accessed here. This is why your Soul Star chakra is so important and why the magenta dragons are seeking out those who are ready to access their soul wisdom. They prepare the way so that the Archangel can wake you up at a deep soul level. They help you on the next step of your journey to merge with your soul or higher self. This is ascension. They accelerate it.

Here is a visualization to connect with the magenta dragons so that you allow the door to your vast soul memories to open. You will sit in the centre of your illumined soul to feel your true light. These dragons will inspire you to be a spiritual light, bringing the planet forward.

This is an excellent visualization to do last thing at night before you sleep.

Visualization to Help You Rediscover Your Soul Wisdom

1. Find a place where you can be quiet and undisturbed.
2. Invoke one of Archangel Mariel's magenta pink dragons.
3. Be aware of this glorious dragon creating a magenta flame round you.

4. It is blowing it into your soul star to fan it to life. See it expand and glow.
5. Above you is the multicoloured flame of your illumined soul.
6. Sit on the dragon's back, as it takes you on a journey to visit other lifetimes, planes of existence and even different universes.
7. You bring back memories, consciously or unconsciously.
8. It flies with you into the centre of the flame that is your vast soul energy.
9. See the colours, the light and energies that are swirling around you.
10. Rest calmly here and notice how you feel.
11. Note how immense and illumined you truly are.
12. The magenta dragon returns you to where you started.
13. Bring your entire soul energy down with you for a few moments.
14. Ask that as much of your higher-self energy stays with you as possible.
15. Thank Archangel Mariel's magenta dragon and open your eyes.

Chapter 4

Quan Yin's Pink Dragons

Quan Yin, the Eastern equivalent of Mother Mary in the West, is known as the Goddess of Mercy. She was and still is very much loved and revered all over the world.

She is a Dragon Master and many thousands of dragons work under her direction. In 2012 at the Cosmic Moment, the dragon portal of Honolulu started to open and her luminous pink dragons poured in to help humanity.

She is often seen by sensitives, travelling with a pink dragon round her shoulders. You may like to consider inviting one of Quan Yin's dragons to wrap itself round your shoulders and feel its energy.

Her etheric retreat is above the glorious mountains of China along the Silk Road, where she spent much of her time, and here her beautiful dragons wait for us to call them to action.

She had a 2000-year incarnation in China and during that long time always expressed pure love, compassion and wisdom. She radiates luminous transcendent pink and occasionally diamond white, and her dragons carry this energy with her. She chose to remain in incarnation for that long period so that she could assist humanity.

The dragons travel with people through the dimensions. When she lived in the fifth dimension she maintained her physical body and stayed healthy by enjoying light food. While her spirit spent time in the seventh dimension, the dragons protected her physical body. They looked after her whenever she travelled through the frequency bands and they also created portals for her to access the ninth dimension.

Many people are becoming multidimensional as the new golden era approaches, even though they may not realize it. If you are one of these, ask Quan Yin's pink dragons to protect you and conduct you through the frequency bands, so that you can maintain a higher vibration for longer.

Once you have connected with Quan Yin's dragons, they will flow and undulate beside you, protecting you and enabling you to circumnavigate your challenges.

The task of Quan Yin's dragons is to help her to maintain her frequency and to pass her knowledge and cosmic understanding on to others. They are bathing us in her light so that we open our consciousness to her special love and deepest wisdom. Then they guide and protect us as they do their beloved Quan Yin.

Spreading Divine Feminine Wisdom

Currently Quan Yin serves on the Intergalactic Council. Her task is to spread divine feminine wisdom, to empower women and influence men to be in touch with their gentler side.

She is also on the Board of Karma, which consists of 12 illumined beings, as Master of the 6th Ray. In this capacity she is helping to bring balance into religion and spirituality.

Under her direction the loving pink dragons breathe her love and wisdom over groups of women and individuals to influence them. They puff light into the minds of teachers to enlighten them. They also breathe energy into the minds of those who are working in traditional male domains in order to expand their consciousness. They try to influence those in charge of businesses or governments or decision-making committees to take wise decisions for the highest good of everyone.

Healing the Sacral Chakras of Humanity

Quan Yin's dragons are trying to heal the sacral chakras of humanity. They are holding the vision of these centres, radiating bright luminous pink transcendent love so that the world can be one again. When they are invited to do this, they go to individuals and families where they blow away or transmute all the lower energies that block people from really loving. They help people to understand the underlying causes of blocks in the sacral chakra, so that humans can truly see with eyes of love. They illuminate situations. They dissolve cords in this chakra and pour light into limiting sexual beliefs. They melt away any old pains, guilt and wounds held here.

When old beliefs and ways of seeing things have been removed, you feel lighter and you treat everyone with respect and love, seeing the best in them. These grace-filled dragons help you to enjoy closer friendships and enriched relationships.

Commanding the Elements

Quan Yin is a Master of the Elements. She can control air, earth, fire and water and is often seen travelling with a dragon of one of the elements. She sends her dragons to subdue huge waves, to calm hurricanes, to quieten earthquakes or to quench fires. When you centre and calm yourself, then stand in your power and send her dragons to soothe situations caused by the elements, you can truly influence the world.

Spirituality and Religion

True spirituality accepts all religions as a path up the spiritual mountain to the oneness of Source. Part of Quan Yin's role is to spread and implement this truth. Her dragons are helping to light up the minds of those ready to embrace this higher understanding.

Visualization to Help You to Heal Your Relationships

1. Find a place where you can be quiet and undisturbed.
2. Invoke Quan Yin's dragons and be aware of these luminous pink light beings round you.
3. Ask them to fill your heart with pure love.
4. Request them to pour their transcendent love into your sacral chakra.
5. Ask them to dissolve any cords in your chakra that tie you to others, from this life or any other, in any dimension or plane of existence.
6. Feel all the karma being dissolved under the Law of Grace.
7. Ask them to heal all your relationships, including those from past lives that you may be unaware of.
8. Ask them to help you to see with eyes of love and see the divine in everyone.
9. Feel yourself wrapped in pink love.
10. Thank the dragons and open your eyes.

Chapter 5

Archangel Gabriel's White Crystal Dragons

Archangel Gabriel is a pure white archangel whose influence spreads over many universes. He brings clarity, joy, hope, purity and self-discipline. He also helps you to understand and heal your relationships. He is in charge of the development of the base, sacral and navel chakras of all sentient beings.

Archangel Gabriel's dragons shimmer with white crystal light. They serve their archangel with love and devotion and their vision is to prepare you to walk the Diamond Ascension Path. When you have enough pure white light in your aura you can walk the Diamond Ascension Path of purity, hope, joy, happiness and love. You will connect with the Great White Brotherhood (*see page* 233), which includes all the organizations that have developed and uphold the pure white truth.

When you are ready to connect more closely with them and with Archangel Gabriel or to open your base, sacral and navel chakras, these pure white dragons will swirl round you. They beam their intense white light into your energy fields, so that clearing and purification can take place. Then they focus on your physical body so that deep cleansing can free your cells to light up. These white dragons can consume any lower vibrations that have been washed out, though they often travel with the Gold and Silver Violet Flame Dragons, who take over and transmute all that is released.

These pure white dragons also have an affinity with the pure white unicorns. If a person or group is working with the unicorns, the dragons will collect the lower energies that are washed out. They will package the muddy vibrations and ask the unicorns to take them into the inner planes where they can be transmuted. The unicorns usually take them to the purest places of the planet, such as above the Himalayas or Mount Shasta (the retreat of Archangel Gabriel) or the mountains of China.

The light of these dragons is so pure that they can illuminate your very essence, until you become spiritually transparent. The effect is rather like holding a dirty cloth up to the light. Every stain becomes visible. They do not judge, nor do any of the beings of the spiritual realms who are watching you with hope and anticipation. They all see how well you are doing in difficult circumstances. Vibrationally, Earth is like a sludgy pond, so it is almost impossible to live on this planet without getting mud on you.

Furthermore, many lightworkers are taking in and transmuting negativity from their ancestral lines as well as the collective karma of humanity. The pure white dragons of Archangel Gabriel are now helping us enormously to prepare ourselves and the planet for the new Golden Age ahead.

These dragons call on you to do some work on yourself, to examine and acknowledge the hurt of your inner child, to explore the source of your patterns and to recognize who you really are. When you have done this, they will illuminate you internally. You may find people comment that you are glowing!

You can then walk the Diamond Ascension Path. Archangel Gabriel's white dragons will move in front of you, clearing and energizing your new higher spiritual path. Now if you move back to a lower muddy path for a time they will surround you and light your way back to the higher one. If someone splashes you with negativity, they will bring you clarity, hope and illumination, so that it falls quickly away from you.

At this point Archangel Gabriel himself will overlight you when you need it, for you will carry his Cosmic Diamond in your energy fields. This will protect your aura and fill you with a sense of happiness and higher purpose.

You will be a beacon, radiating a pure white light to show others the way. People will sense your light and will react to it according to their beliefs or fears. Some may even see or sense Archangel Gabriel's shimmering white dragons as they swirl round you, protecting and illuminating you.

You will be clearly visible to the spiritual realms.

Exercise to Become a Beacon of Light

1. Call the dragons to you and sense, see or imagine them lighting you up internally with a million tiny white lights.
2. Sense, see or imagine them placing a vast cosmic diamond over your aura.
3. Know that you are a beacon of light as you go about your day.

Visualization to Prepare You to Walk the Diamond Ascension Path

1. Find a place where you can be quiet and undisturbed.
2. Light a candle if possible and dedicate it to the diamond-white dragons lighting you up internally.
3. Close your eyes and relax.
4. See, sense or imagine sparkling white dragons swirling round you.
5. Be aware of beams of light from their hearts, lasering into you.
6. Feel lower energies washing out of your cells and forming a pool of mud by your feet.
7. The mud is collected by a pristine white unicorn, who takes it away to be transmuted.
8. Sense your cells becoming clearer and purer.
9. Now Archangel Gabriel's dragons illuminate you – every cell of your body shimmers with pure sparkling white light.
10. Instantly a cosmic diamond surrounds your aura.
11. The beautiful Diamond Ascension Path appears in front of you and the dragons surround you as you walk along it.
12. You are a beacon of light showing others the way.
13. Enjoy the feeling and know the spiritual realms are watching over you.
14. Thank the dragons and open your eyes.

Chapter 6

Archangel Raphael's Emerald Dragons

The emerald dragons work with Archangel Raphael, the emerald archangel of healing and abundance. Archangel Raphael operates between the seventh- and ninth-dimensional frequencies. He holds the blueprint of your perfect health and, if your soul permits it, tries to raise your vibration above that of the illness. Then the dis-ease has to dissolve.

The emerald dragons are fifth-dimensional and hold a spiritual vision of your perfect health, but they see the lower thoughts, emotions or beliefs from past lives, ancestral karma or soul blocks that are stuck in your energy fields causing the dis-ease. If your soul allows it, they dive in and try to consume the lower vibrations.

So, the dragons and angels work differently but with a common purpose.

Abundance Consciousness

The emerald dragons and Archangel Raphael also work together in a similar way to raise your level of abundance consciousness. If you are living your life with love and integrity, in a fifth-dimensional way, they help your third eye to develop. There are 96 petals or chambers in this very sensitive chakra. Archangel Raphael's angels take every opportunity to raise the frequency within the chambers by presenting you with the lessons contained in them, while the emerald dragons plunge in to clear and transmute stuck energy.

When your third eye is open, spinning and radiating, the angels help you build a shaft of light up to the cosmic third eye, which is Jupiter and its aspect Jumbay, which has already ascended. Jumbay literally means vast, expansive, all encompassing, enlightened. Here, a true understanding of cosmic abundance is stored. While the dragons of Jupiter protect the wisdom held here, the emerald dragons look after it as it pours down the shaft of light into your third eye. It fills the chambers of your third eye with abundance consciousness that contains a true belief in your deservingness and an absolute knowledge that you can access all that you need, which will be provided for you in a perfect way.

Because this information is so sacred and desirable, the emerald dragons protect your third eye so that no one can draw it from you.

The Chakra of Enlightenment

Your third eye is the chakra of enlightenment, the ability to see everything from a higher, wider, divine perspective. Many people are currently not ready to see with enlightened eyes and so the emerald dragons also protect your third eye from those who would access it.

The Key to Clairvoyance

This powerful chakra holds the key to clairvoyance, clear-seeing through the veils of illusion. When the chambers holding these codes are open you can see in glorious radiant colour what is happening in other dimensions. You may see dragons, unicorns, angels, fairies, spirits of Illumined Masters and many beautiful things. You may also tune in to dark and undesirable entities. These particular chambers may remain closed because of past-life trauma. Many clear-sighted people were put to death for their powers and the residue of fear keeps part of this chakra firmly closed. If you want to open the doors, ask the emerald dragons to help you.

Cleansing and Polishing the Third Eye

During live-streaming on Facebook one time, I was suddenly impressed to do a third-eye cleanse and polish for everyone watching. I called in the air-and-water dragons to wash and then blow-dry the chambers of the third eye. Then, I asked Archangel Raphael to polish the lens of the third eye. The emerald dragons protected the chakra while the work was being done.

Next day I had an email from Birkan Tore, who is a wonderful clairvoyant. He wrote, 'The third-eye clearing and polishing worked wonders for me. My third eye was so tired and overworked that it really needed some special attention. The combination of air-and-water dragons *and* Archangel Raphael was exactly what was needed. It was one of the most tangible and effective healing meditations I've ever experienced. The next day I woke up with a sense of calm right within my third eye and my clairvoyant work felt simply effortless.'

Visualization to Cleanse and Polish the Third Eye

1. Find a place where you can be quiet and undisturbed.
2. Take a moment to breathe gently in and out of your third eye.
3. Visualize your third eye as a spiral with 96 chambers.
4. Invoke the emerald dragons and ask them to enter your chakra and puff emerald-green light into each chamber where the door is open.
5. If a door is closed ask what lies behind. You may want to ask the dragons to open it and clear old stuff or bring forward treasures. Use your intuition about whether or not to do so.
6. Ask Archangel Raphael to link your chakra to Jupiter and Jumbay, and sense the shaft of light connecting them, in place.
7. The emerald dragons are swirling round the shaft of light, protecting the keys and codes of abundance consciousness now coming into your third eye.
8. Relax and absorb what you are ready for.
9. Thank the emerald dragons and Archangel Raphael.

Chapter 7

Archangel Jophiel's Crystal Yellow Dragons

Your crown chakra, the spiritual centre above your head, has a thousand petals or chambers and is often called the thousand-petalled lotus. Your chakra of wisdom, it holds the Christ light of unconditional love. When this chakra is anchored and open, the pale golden petals start to unfurl. They reach out and link into the various cosmic energies of the universe. This includes planets, stars, numbers or pools of light.

Archangel Jophiel, the Angel of Wisdom, is in charge of the development of the crown chakra of humanity and animals. It is incredibly important. Not only does it link into the universal energies but, when it is fully open, the light and wisdom held in the three transcendent chakras above the head start to flow down through the spiritual energy system of the body. You move into a higher spiritual level of understanding. It is a step to becoming a Cosmic Master.

A Being of the Universe

One of the tasks of Archangel Jophiel's beautiful crystal yellow dragons is to swirl round the crown and keep this chakra pure and clear. Each petal vibrates with a specific energy and when this attunes to that of an energy of the universe, it starts to open. The crystal yellow dragons cleanse each petal and untangle it, if necessary. They blow away any old energies holding it back, especially the very common belief of not being good enough. Another belief from past-life experiences that stops many lightworkers from revealing their true self is the fear that they will be incarcerated or put to death if their light is seen. Such ideas belong to the past and the crystal yellow dragons are working hard to free us from limiting beliefs provoked by past-life experiences. They then strengthen and light up that petal, so it can reach out and connect as appropriate.

As the petals start to grow and link into universal energies, you become a Being of the Universe, as you recognize that you are part of something much greater than your little self on Earth.

The dragons protect and strengthen these links to the universe and help you integrate the light containing spiritual information and knowledge. They cooperate with the glorious pure unicorns to connect you into many sources of universal wisdom and knowledge.

Fifth-dimensional Wisdom Codes

The crystal yellow dragons carry fifth-dimensional wisdom codes for the universe and can download them into you when you are ready. They open you to higher learnings. They illuminate your crown, bringing forward your majestic light as well as your connections. This enables you to walk the Diamond Ascension Path where you can be a beacon for others.

When the huge, open-hearted crystal yellow dragons have illuminated the entire crown chakra to a fifth-dimensional frequency, it glows so that the heavenly realms can see you. And when you connect with them, it is time for you to walk a higher spiritual path.

The dragons remind you that you are a Being of the Universe. The ultimate is to become a Cosmic Master and step onto a diamond path. The crystal yellow dragons will ensure you connect with those who are ready for the light you carry. When you meet these people, your light will automatically light up the keys and codes of mastery latent within them.

Archangel Jophiel's crystal yellow dragons are especially drawn to those who are prepared to let their light be seen. When they have illuminated and expanded the crown chakras of these particular people, their light will automatically ignite the keys and codes of universal wisdom latent within the crown chakras of others. This will enable the planet to ascend more quickly.

The time is now for this higher service.

Exercise to Help You Link in to the Wisdom of the Universe

1. Stand outside on a starry night.
2. Imagine your crown chakra ignited and the thousand petals reaching up to connect with the stars.
3. Sense Archangel Jophiel's crystal yellow dragons helping them to link into the wisdom of the universe at a rate that you can accept.
4. Be still and centred while the universe works its magic.

Visualization to Open the Petals of Your Crown Chakra

1. Find a place where you can be quiet and undisturbed.
2. Light a candle and dedicate it to the opening of the petals of your crown chakra.
3. Focus on your crown chakra and sense the energy there.
4. Call in Archangel Jophiel's crystal yellow dragons and sense or see them swirling round the top of your head, cleansing and lighting up the petals.
5. Visualize your crown with the thousand petals starting to wake up and unfurl.
6. Sense one of the petals reaching up, while a crystal yellow dragon puffs air round it to free and cleanse it.
7. Be aware of the dragon illuminating it, so that the petal shimmers with Christ light.
8. Tune in to this petal and sense where it is linking to – maybe a star or a particular ball of energy?
9. Sense the link being made and new cosmic light and wisdom pouring back into your crown chakra.
10. See the crystal yellow dragons protecting the wonderful new energy in your crown.
11. Relax and allow the energy to integrate.
12. Thank the crystal yellow dragons and open your eyes.

Chapter 8

Archangel Michael's Deep Blue Dragons

Archangel Michael is the great, deep blue angel of strength and protection in charge of the throat chakras of humanity. His powerful dragons work with him to bring strength, protection and inspiration to people everywhere.

Firing You with Strength and Courage

These blue dragons can fire you up with courage and the strength to stand for what you believe in. They will build an etheric firewall to protect you from flak that might come back from those who do not want you to stand in your power. This is really empowering for anyone who has become a victim or been downtrodden; to them, Archangel Michael offers inspiration and a vision of who they truly can be. His dragons can burn up fear and negativity that has kept them stuck in a relentless pattern.

The great archangel can give you his Sword of Truth to strengthen your resolve and encourage you, while his deep blue dragons can clear your pathway and transmute the lower frequencies.

Archangel Michael can offer you his deep blue Cloak of Protection, to ensure that your aura is strong enough to repel other people's judgements and criticisms, or worse. The dragons can burn up the lower vibrations of those judgements, criticisms or attacking thoughts, so that they do not reach you. Together they are great protectors.

Clearing the Area Around You

When you visit a shopping mall or any crowded place, you are in a sea of mixed vibrations. The emotions and thoughts of everyone there are washing through you if you are sensitive or wide open. If someone else's problems or fears invade your energy field, you may feel drained, exhausted or even desperate.

Dragons can delve into deep dense matter in a way that angels cannot. Archangel Michael's deep blue dragons are master clearance experts. They can clear and transmute lower frequencies up to one kilometre (just over half a mile) around those they work with. They remind us that, when we humans take responsibility for our thoughts, words and lower emotions, the planet will be a lighter, brighter place.

By definition a path of light is clear. You can ask these dragons to keep you safe by blowing away and transmuting any fog that blurs your clear view or any mud that impedes you. Then you can move forward with confidence.

Protecting You and Your Loved Ones

Archangel Michael's deep blue dragons often work together, like a protecting army. You can call on them to protect you at any time. Just think of them gliding in front of you to your workplace and staying on duty all day. Imagine them as sentries round your home. As soon as you have the thought, they will be there.

You can ask them to surround and look after your loved ones or any individual or group of people, even a nation that is in need.

Clearing the Ground

When you invite an army of Archangel Michael's deep blue dragons to dive under your home or office to clear all lower energies, you may feel an instant lightening, because they are very powerful. Dense clouds of negativity float everywhere. You can serve the planet by asking the deep blue warrior dragons to visit your shopping mall, schools, big buildings or anywhere they are needed, and consume the clouds.

Visualization to Clear the Space Around You

1. Find a place where you can be quiet and undisturbed.
2. Light a candle and dedicate it to working with Archangel Michael's deep blue dragons.
3. Invoke an army of these dragons and sense or see them sweeping towards you.
4. As rank upon rank of deep blue dragons stand in front of you, sense their power.
5. Ask them to sweep under your home, and notice how you feel afterwards.
6. Do the same for your work place, your shopping mall or supermarket, train station, airport, schools, government offices or any other building.
7. Ask the dragons to clear a space of a kilometre (just over half a mile) round you. Notice how it feels to walk in clear energy.
8. Visualize yourself walking on a path of light carrying a beacon to show others the way.
9. Thank Archangel Michael's deep blue dragons and find yourself back where you started.

Chapter 9

Archangel Fhelyai's Sunshine Yellow Dragons

Archangel Fhelyai's sunshine yellow dragons are the most gentle and compassionate of all the dragons. They shelter animals under their wings to support and comfort them. They help them with their soul missions because, just like us, each animal has a purpose in incarnating. Like us, they come from a variety of star systems and planets in this and other universes and are invited for this experience on Earth to learn, experience, teach and serve.

Do Elementals Help Animals?

Many years ago, I asked my guide Kumeka if elementals helped animals – for example: if a dog was lost, would a fairy or other elemental step forward to help it find its way? I was told that this would not happen, as elementals and animals did not really connect. That changed, like so many things, in 2012.

Archangel Fhelyai stepped through from another universe to help the animals on Earth ascend. He also arrived in response to their cries for assistance. The extraordinary level of disconnect that occurred between humans and the animals we are supposed to look after was never envisaged.

Archangel Fhelyai brought thousands of his sunshine yellow dragons with him and their focus and intent is to help the animal kingdom. Part of this is to help humans understand our fellow creatures, because when we realize who they truly are, we will be in awe of them and respect them. The curriculum for us to ascend includes understanding and honouring the animal kingdom. When you really love animals, the sunshine yellow dragons blow their light into your energy fields. Eventually, sunshine yellow will become a permanent colour in your aura and you will radiate it. You will also feel much happier.

How the Sunshine Yellow Dragons Help Animals

The sunshine yellow dragons are trying very hard to pull unhelpful beliefs out of the consciousness of those who do not yet know how to treat all creatures with respect. There are still many on Earth who think animals are unfeeling commodities rather than living, breathing, intelligent, feeling spirits in a body of flesh as we are. They have been given a different shape from us and a different life purpose, but essentially we are all divine beings.

Most humans are here to experience life through the left brain and the intellect. Most animals are here to experience it through the right brain and the heart.

As with all things in this plane of free will, dragons cannot interfere with someone's karma without permission. We can, however, create a bridge of light to that person from our hearts and minds and ask the dragons to send their energy along the bridge of light to them. When enough people ask Archangel Fhelyai and his dragons to go to owners of abattoirs or factory farms or gangs of poachers, there will be change. The archangel can surround those unaware people with sunshine yellow light to raise their consciousness, while the dragons can pour in light containing the keys and codes to enable them to understand the purpose of the animals. At the same time, the dragons can burn up the lower beliefs that allow people to treat creatures in the way that they do.

There are many humans who need to change their relationship with animals.

Making a Portal for Animals

Sometimes at workshops I ask everyone to contribute energy to creating a portal of light. On one occasion we all created a sunshine yellow portal for the animals of the world. We held the intention that it would be a place of refuge and comfort for the spirits of animals, as well as a place where they can pass over more easily.

We then asked the earth dragons to ground the portal and hold it in position for as long as it was needed, while the sunshine yellow dragons of Archangel Fhelyai swirled round it, protecting it.

As soon as we had finished, a host of hands went up as participants described what they saw. I was quite taken aback as I had seen rhinos, brought by their guardian angels, coming into the portal and we were in the UK. The others shared that they had seen elephants, giraffe, zebras and a whole host of African animals. It demonstrated that those animals needed the energy and that distance was of no importance.

The next to arrive were animals killed on the roads, who had died in shock and were looking for the light. They, too, dived into the sunshine yellow comfort.

A clairvoyant then shared that she had seen the portal forming about 2 metres (2 yards) wide. As soon as the dragons were called in to protect it, the portal doubled in width and the colour became brighter and deeper.

Together we created a high-frequency refuge for many animals in need. I wonder if people using the hall in future will be surprised if they see or sense a lion in that corner!

You can ask that the spirits of people who need to change their attitude to animals are brought here by their guardian angels to absorb higher understandings.

Build a portal in a group, if possible, as combined energy is exponentially more powerful than a single focus. Also, you may prefer to combine your light with people you may not know to create a portal in a particular place in the world – for example, on the Holy Island, Scotland, which is Archangel Fhelyai's retreat. If enough people add energy, this will make a significant impact.

Visualization to Build a Portal for Animals

1. Decide on a safe area to place the portal. It can be outside or inside, but preferably somewhere quiet where the energies of too many people do not impact on it. If in doubt, focus on the Holy Island, Scotland.
2. Decide on the purpose of the gateway to higher frequencies that you are creating. Is it to provide a light path for animals to pass through when they die or a place where they can find refuge or healing? Or is it a place where angels can bring the spirits of humans who need to understand the animal kingdom? Or a place where all these things are combined? State the purpose.
3. Invoke Archangel Fhelyai to send his angels here to create a column of sunshine yellow light. Raise your hands, directed towards the portal, and let the yellow light pour through them to build it.
4. Ask the earth dragons to ground and anchor the portal and set a time limit for it, if you wish.
5. Ask the sunshine yellow dragons to circle round the shaft of light to help construct and to protect it.
6. You may like to wait for a while to sense what animals or people arrive to use the portal.
7. Visualize the animals entering the portal and being lit up with hope.
8. See the minds and hearts of the people blazing glorious yellow as they expand their perspective and see animals for who they truly are.
9. Relax and know your heart is opening and you are accruing good karma.

Chapter 10

Archangel Metatron's Golden Orange Dragons

The golden orange dragons work on Archangel Metatron's team to accelerate your personal ascension and that of the planet, as well as the entire universe's! At the Cosmic Moment, at 11:11 a.m. on 21 December 2012, the light of Source touched the heart of every sentient being in every universe. It was a trigger. At that instant a movement towards ascension to a higher frequency was set off everywhere. Each universe is on a 20-year journey into a new dimension. Of all the stars and planets, only Earth has fallen behind and has to step up two dimensions. We are proving a little challenging as seven billion souls crowd in to clear a backlog of karma before the deadline of 2032. At the same time, we are relentlessly insisting on using our gift of free will.

The earthly equivalent would be the end of a school year when all the classes are moving up a grade except one class. That one has fallen so far behind it has to catch up an additional grade. Nearly all the pupils have missed lessons and need extra teaching. So, an intense process is under way to see that every pupil is ready for the shift.

Archangel Metatron is in charge of this progression. The more we call on his golden orange dragons, the more will arrive to support us.

Helping Our Ascension Journey

It is the dragons who help us travel through the dimensional levels. Millions of them, of every colour, size and shape, from various planets and stars, even from different dimensions, are pouring forward now to assist with this current interdimensional shift.

The golden orange dragons who work for Archangel Metatron carry the fifth-dimensional ascension blueprint for Earth. They know the proposed flight path for every single individual to 2032. They offer you protection, encouragement and inspiration, and strengthen your willpower. They understand your gifts, talents and potential. If you need more tuition, they can guide you towards special tutors who can help you. You only have to ask.

They light your way as soon as they see you are ready. Then these dragons breathe glorious ascension light into you and this draws illumined masters, higher guides, angels and unicorns to you. They all work together to accelerate your spiritual journey. When the golden orange flame appears in your energy fields they know you are also prepared and willing to help others onto the ascension path. You are a Master.

Ask yourself what you need in order to accelerate your ascension. Do you need to develop qualities? To meditate more? Or to commit yourself to your path? Or to have faith in yourself? Or just to enjoy life and have more fun? Ask the golden orange dragons to light those qualities in you, and to help you to embrace your magnificence.

Releasing Unhelpful Beliefs to Free Your Ascension Pathway

The golden orange dragons help you to dissolve the beliefs that hold you back. Almost every human holds them. Some lightworkers undertake to bring in beliefs from the collective unconscious that are holding humanity back in the old age. They do this as an act of service in order to help the world by releasing them. Clearing beliefs that impact on their personal lives becomes their great challenge. Others are taking on ancestral beliefs, with the intention of dissolving them to free their entire family tree and future generations. Archangel Metatron's golden orange dragons can really help you clear these.

So, take time to consider what beliefs stop you from being an Ascended Master. Any that are not in alignment with love, oneness and your own divine magnificence need to be pulled out and cleared. Some are great thick cords linking back to past lives or even past collective karma. Others are more delicate or tenuous, but they all have an influence on your ascension journey. Then, ask Archangel Metatron's golden orange dragons to breathe into them and help you to dissolve them.

Planetary Ascension

Archangel Metatron's dragons are peaceful warriors. They are the spiritual lights that patrol the universe ensuring everything is as it should be. They teach humanity by example, demonstrating spirituality, peace, love and wisdom. At the same time, they can breathe fire and roar when it is needed!

The Metatron Cloak

Archangel Metatron gives you his golden orange cloak when your 12 fifth-dimensional chakras are awake. The energy of the cloak helps to keep them open and the dragons assist in keeping lower entities at bay. They literally chase away or burn up any negativity that is trying to undermine you. One of the most important gifts, the Metatron Cloak, gives you is the desire and ability to reach out and help others onto the ascension path.

When you wear the golden orange cloak in your energy fields, you can enter Hollow Earth, which is the seventh-dimensional chakra in the centre of the planet. You do this in meditation or sleep and these glorious dragons will conduct you to the Great Pyramid in the middle of Hollow Earth. Here all the knowledge and wisdom of Earth is contained, so when you are quiet and centred, you can soak it in. In the centre of the Pyramid you can align to the portals that link to the four ascension constellations and planets: the Pleiades, Orion, Sirius and Neptune, to draw in light from these heavenly bodies.

Archangel Metatron's dragons will protect you on this journey that will greatly accelerate your ascension.

Exercise to Release Old Beliefs and Free up Your Ascension Path

1. Write down how you would be if you were an Illumined Ascended Master.
2. List any beliefs that prevent you from being one.
3. Imagine how big each of these beliefs is and see it shrinking.
4. Draw a golden orange bubble round each one and ask Metatron's dragons to help you to dissolve them.
5. Write down positive beliefs that will help your ascension path.

Visualization to Meet Archangel Metatron and Visit Hollow Earth

1. Find a place where you can be quiet and undisturbed, and imagine that a glorious, radiant golden orange dragon is standing in front of you.
2. You ride on its back, through the dimensions, to Archangel Metatron's vast etheric retreat above Luxor.
3. Here Archangel Metatron, glowing with light, places his golden orange cloak over your energy fields. If you have already received it, he re-activates it.
4. Receive his blessings.
5. Your dragon flies with you to the portal leading to Hollow Earth. As you plunge through it together you become one vast golden orange flame.
6. You see the Great Pyramid of Hollow Earth and enter it on your dragon.
7. Sitting, quiet and still, in the centre of the pyramid, you are aligned to Neptune, the Pleiades, Orion and Sirius. You are open to receive the light codes that pour down into you from each place.
8. Rest here. Know and trust that your ascension light is expanding.
9. The dragon takes you gently out of the pyramid and up through the portal again.
10. It takes you to a vast cosmic mirror and invites you to see your divine magnificence.
11. Then it returns you to where you started. Thank it and know you will meet again.

PART V

Galactic Dragons

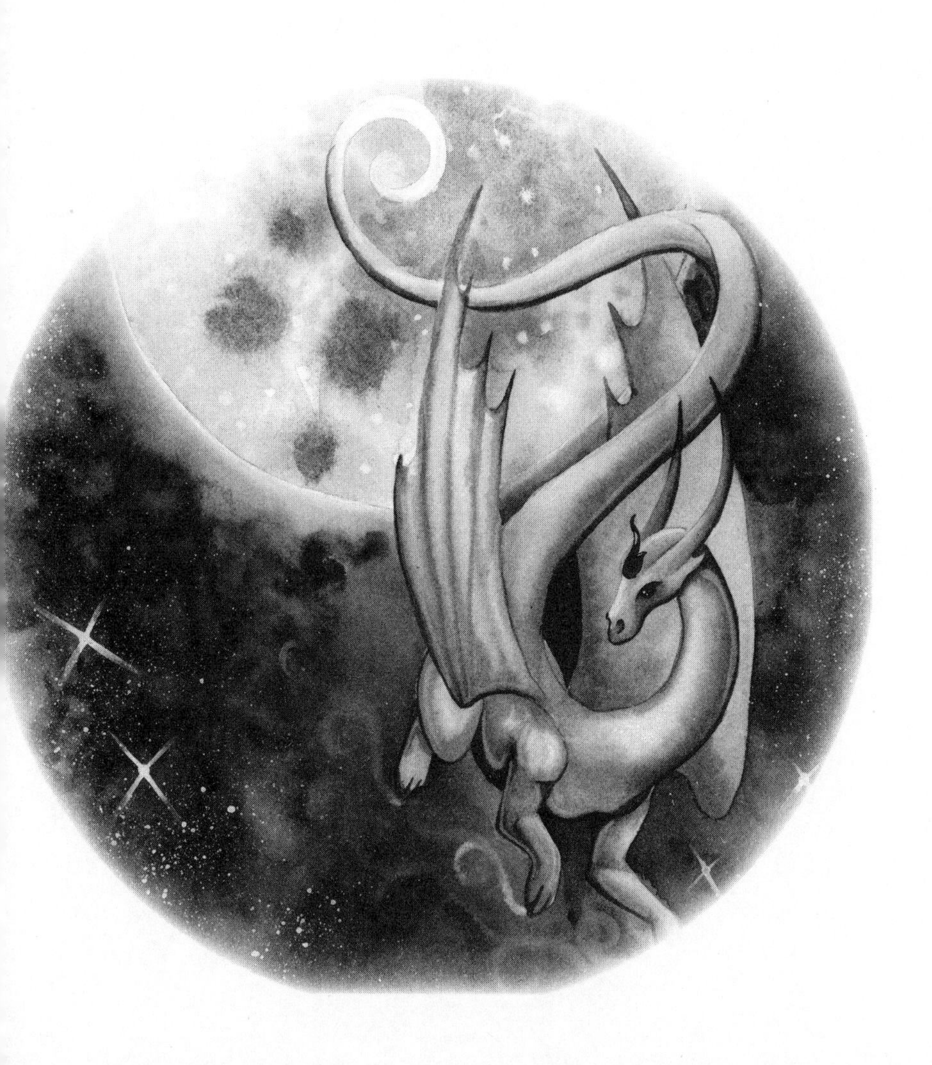

Introduction

The galactic dragons come from the stars or planets in this universe and carry very high frequencies and incredible wisdom. The ancients of the Golden Era of Atlantis used to connect to the stars to bring back stellar wisdom and this helped to take the civilization into the extraordinary ascension it achieved. Since 2015 these incredible high-frequency spiritual beings have been able to connect with humans and are once more sharing their light with us.

There is much more to you than your physical body. Your soul exists in many planes and dimensions and there may be many aspects of yourself that you are not aware of. If you are reading this you may well be an Intergalactic Master in the inner planes or aspire to become one. In that case you will have an immediate rapport with these galactic dragons and be open to their downloads of knowledge and wisdom. Even if you have no galactic aspirations, these dragons can open you up to new understanding and higher light. In addition, dragons from different stars or galaxies can touch specific chakras with energies and codes that develop them to a much higher level than we have thought possible.

Chapter 1

Dusky Pink Dragons from Andromeda

These beautiful dragons radiate a soft, luminous pink light. They carry the frequency of transcendent love. When these dragons touch you, they enable you to see the good in others, to connect for an instant with the true light of their souls. When you see the genuine love and light that is the essence of someone, something pure flashes between you. At the deepest level a seed of acceptance and understanding is planted. It may take time for that seed to develop and grow. However, these great shining dragons from Andromeda are undertaking a monumental task on Earth to heal old separations and bring about pure love. They are working with individuals, families, communities and countries. You can help them.

Different Frequencies of Love

The dusky pink dragons from Andromeda plant a flame of pure love in each of your 12 chakras, which illuminates your aura with a lovely, soft pink glow. This prepares all your chakras to receive higher love. Then you can touch others with the flame of transcendent love. This pink flame carries many frequencies of love and light, for there are many shades of pink, each with a special energy. So, you can ignite and transform many different souls with exactly the right frequency of love. They may not even be aware of it but they will feel better. Their hearts may feel softer, their fears lessened, their viewpoints transformed. Change may be subtle but you will be spreading it when you work with these magical dragons.

All the stars in the constellation of Andromeda embody a beautiful love and acceptance beyond our current understanding. They radiate this energy and the dragons are their emissaries who take it out into the universe. They naturally cooperate with the Angels of Andromeda, Archangel Chamuel, Archangel Mariel and Illumined Dragon Masters such as Quan Yin to spread the various frequencies of their love.

Pale white-pink radiates a pure soothing energy. The pink of cherry blossom opens the heart and this tree blossoms in the spring to prepare those who see it for innocent or romantic love. Blue-pink carries an artistic vibration, while deep pink brings creativity. Every shade is subtly distinctive and affects us in a unique way. The dragons of Andromeda can activate them all and know exactly what they are doing.

Crickets

The beings from Andromeda have the shape of crickets. I was talking to the most gracious and gentle, very creative gay man, who had just discovered that he came from Andromeda. He was surprised to find himself in the etheric body of a cricket. But all beings as well as all animals are spirits in different-shaped bodies and there is a huge diversity of creatures out in the universe. So, it is not surprising that the dusky pink dragons work with the crickets and grasshoppers, who come from their constellation.

The song of the crickets, made by rubbing their legs together, is extraordinary. When slowed down it sounds like a heavenly cathedral choir and the music carries the codes of higher love.

Bathing You in Love

The mission of all beings from this constellation is to bathe all those who are ready to receive it in the vibration of transcendent love.

The dragons are patiently waiting for people who are ready for their light to call them. You can ask them to bathe the chambers within your chakras with their dusky pink light, which carries all the frequencies of love.

More about the Chakras

The Earth Star chakra contains 33 chambers, each of which holds lessons about honouring the Earth.

The base chakra has two chambers, each devoted to living in a grounded, spiritually disciplined way and bringing your life into masculine–feminine balance.

In the third-dimensional chakra column, the sacral and navel chakras combine, though the petals of the navel are closed. When your 12 chakras descend, the sacral and navel separate. Each has 16 chambers. Those in the translucent pink sacral chakra hold the keys of sexual and emotional balance, while the bright orange navel keeps the codes of artistic and creative expression. These contain the secrets of manifestation. The 33rd chakra is a huge chamber that encompasses all the 32 rooms.

The solar plexus contains 33 chambers. As you enter and learn from each one, you take a journey to wisdom and finally to becoming an Intergalactic Master.

The 33 chambers of the heart chakra enable you to develop from self-centredness through to oneness.

The throat chakra is very sensitive and its 22 chambers take you on a learning curve from human dishonesty to trust in God.

There are 96 chambers in the third eye chakra, as this is a huge seat of learning. You transform from ignorance to all-knowing.

The 1000 petals of the lotus of the crown chakra are really portals or gateways to the 1000 vibrational frequencies of God.

The causal chakra is a single chamber of peace that allows you entry into the silence and stillness of the higher mind. The unicorns work here to help it to become quiet, so that it can open fully to enable light from your soul star to come down into your mental body.

The Soul Star chakra consists of a lower part with 33 chambers, then a higher part which blazes out the light of your soul.

The twelfth chakra, the Stellar Gateway, is pure gold and holds the energy of your Monad, which is your true divine essence.

Exercise to Fill Your Chakras with Love

Before you start you need to draw a body on a piece of paper. It can be a pin figure if you wish, but make it as large as possible. If you really want to put a lot of energy into this you can get a roll of paper, such as leftover wallpaper, and lie on it. Then ask your partner or a friend to draw round your body so that you have an outline of yourself.

Next, find a pink flower such as a rose. If possible, pick up 12 petals that have fallen. If you cannot do this, ask the flower if you may pick it and use its petals. Do this with respect.

If you cannot find a flower, be creative instead. Use pieces of pink material or tissue paper. Draw pink flowers and cut them out or make something else that is meaningful to you to represent the 12 chakras.

Now begin the exercise.

1. Find a quiet place and, if possible, light a candle.
2. Starting at the Earth Star Chakra, place a pink petal, or whatever you have created, in the appropriate place on the paper. Overlap the petals, if necessary. Then move up through the 12 chakras, one by one, placing the petals, or whatever you created, on the chakras.
3. Mentally or aloud call in the dusky pink dragons of Andromeda.
4. Focus on each chakra in turn and ask the dragons to enter the chakra you are focusing on and fill the chambers with transcendent love.
5. Think about each chakra and what needs to be lit up within it.
6. When you have reached the Stellar Gateway and finished working on it, draw a pink flame round the body.
7. Thank the dusky pink dragons of Andromeda and know something has ignited within you.

Visualization to Activate and Balance Your Chakras

1. Find a place where you can be quiet and undisturbed.
2. If possible prepare you space with pink crystals, flowers, a candle or whatever you need to raise the energy.
3. Close your eyes and relax. If any part of you needs to let go, breathe into it so that the dragons can access your chakras.
4. Mentally or aloud call in the dusky pink dragons of Andromeda.
5. Be quiet and still. Sense the dragons arriving and circling round you, radiating pink love to you.
6. Now focus on your Earth Star chakra. Visualize the doors to the 33 chambers opening. Let the dragons breathe pink love into each chamber. Ask that any lessons you still need to learn about honouring the Earth are brought forward into your life with love.
7. Shift your awareness to the base chakra and imagine the dragons pouring pink love into both chambers bringing your masculine and feminine energy into balance.
8. Imagine the sacral chakra and, in your mind's eye, see the dragons pouring pink love into the 16 chambers, harmonizing your sexual and emotional balance.

9. Focus on the navel chakra and visualize the dragons pouring pink love into its 16 chambers, lighting up the codes of artistic and creative expression.
10. Imagine the vast 33rd chamber that encompasses all the 32 rooms of the combined sacral and navel chakras, radiating pink joy.
11. Be aware of the solar plexus and see the dragons filling the 33 chambers with love, so that you take with love the journey to wisdom and becoming an Intergalactic Master.
12. Focus on the heart centre and visualize the dragons filling each of the 33 chambers with love, so that you dissolve separation and live in oneness.
13. Shift your awareness to the 22 chambers of the throat chakra as the dragons fill them with love to accelerate your journey to trust in God.
14. At the third eye chakra, the dragons are pausing while the doors to the 96 rooms are allowed to open. Then they gently puff pink light into them, to fill your journey to all-knowing with love.
15. Relax your crown chakra, as you picture the 1000 gateways at your crown open to the 1000 vibrational frequencies of God. Let the dragons pour love into each one to enable you to connect with love.
16. Be very still as the dragons fill the peace chamber of your causal chakra with love.
17. Access the lower part of the Soul Star chakra and let the dragons fill the 33 chambers with love.

Then move up to the higher part and see the luminous pink that is blazing out with the light of your soul.

18. The dragons from Andromeda are rising above your chakra column and pouring white-pink love into the chalice of your Stellar Gateway chakra.
19. Your energy fields have become a pink flame.
20. Thank the dusky pink dragons from Andromeda and merge into the Cosmic Pink Flame they hold over you.

There is more information about the chambers of the chakras and what the journey through each one entails in *Ascension Through Orbs* by Diana Cooper and Kathy Crosswell.

Chapter 2

Aquamarine Dragons from Neptune

The planet Neptune has an incredibly high frequency for here the keys and codes of advanced spirituality for this universe are held.

The Wisdom of Lemuria

The wisdom of the golden angels of Lemuria and Atlantis is also stored here. This is protected by the aquamarine dragons of Neptune. These beautiful dragons also spread the wisdom to those who are ready to receive it.

Lemuria was the Golden Age preceding Atlantis. It was an era when the beings did not have fully physical bodies. They were etheric, so there was no boundary between the individual beings. Rather they were a collective energy, who were guided by the group consciousness. The easiest way to describe how they operated is to talk about migrating birds like swallows, who still carry the wisdom of Lemuria. Swallows are part of a group consciousness. If one moves, they all move. Together they have a single vision and intention. They form a group and take it in turns to guide the way. There is no leader, no ego, no competition, no better than. One is in front. When the time is right, another seamlessly moves forward and takes its place. This saves energy and creates oneness. Their vision is encoded within them, so they all aim for it in the same way that our blueprint ensures that we walk and talk.

Because they were all one, they were very psychic and intuitively knew what the others were feeling. They could also tune in to our planet and know what would be happening in the distant future.

As there was no separation, there was no possession. Everything was shared. They gave and received in a constant flow of abundance. There was no taking, for giving was spontaneous and instant. They saw only love and total trust, for there was only oneness.

Another aspect of Lemurian wisdom was the incredible love they had for Earth, humanity and nature. They tuned in to the hearts of trees, mountains, animals and all the cornucopia of joys we have in this plane of the universe and had the ability to be in total harmony with them. Whenever they focused on anything, they lit it up with pure love, rather as the swallows light up the ley lines over which they fly when they migrate. They lived according to divine feminine principles.

Although they ensouled the wisdom of oneness, the Lemurians had a huge longing to live in a human body and experience this physical plane as we humans do. It was this desire that led to the experiment of Atlantis, when beings took physical bodies.

The Wisdom of Atlantis

The wisdom of the Golden Era of Atlantis was slightly different because the people had bodies, which they knew were a sheath for their spirits. Not only did they have to sustain their flesh, but they had to master emotions and thoughts that affected their physical state. And, in order to experience an incarnation, they had to develop the ability to keep their masculine and feminine aspects in balance. They acted on the spiritual laws, so that they did not create karma. In addition to following the Laws of Oneness, they learned to control their minds so that they could manifest things for the highest good of all. They connected to beings from other star systems, as well as angels, unicorns and dragons, and listened to their advice. Utilizing this wisdom enabled them to take the leap of consciousness that brought about the golden era.

Spreading the Wisdom of the Universe

Neptune is a watery planet and the dragons from here are water dragons. Ask them to take you to bathe in the aquamarine cosmic ocean. Let them touch you with the pure divine feminine wisdom of the Lemurian era and help you to come into balance. Also ask them to awaken within you the higher spiritual laws that were actioned in golden Atlantis, so that you can start to bring back their powerful understandings and amazing spiritual technology.

When you are ready to call them, the aquamarine dragons from Neptune will float round you and download their light into your energy fields. This will activate the keys and codes of the deepest spiritual information and knowledge you have in your soul. Some of this is protected and locked away because, until recently, it was not permitted for anyone to bring forward anything that could do harm if used indiscriminately or without understanding the consequences. These dragons ensure you have the wisdom to use such light and power only for the highest good. So, if you are not ready, nothing will be revealed.

However, because the general consciousness is now higher, it is usually considered safe to allow knowledge to come forward. Your spiritual task is to pass it to others with modesty and integrity.

Waking Your Psychic Abilities Through the Chakras

The aquamarine dragons from Neptune can wake up your psychic abilities, which are latent within all of us. They create a vortex of aquamarine energy and funnel it into the chakras. They enable the chakras to open more easily and raise their frequency for psychic work. Here's how they affect the chakras:

Sacral Chakra

Earlier generations used to say, 'I can feel it in my waters' meaning that their sacral chakra was tuning in to something. When your sacral chakra is sensitive and finely tuned you are clairsentient. Often your bladder tenses up, telling you that you need to be careful. Take notice of it and ask the aquamarine dragons to calm the chakra and help you deal with the situation or person you are being warned about. When you are clairsentient you feel the feelings of others, so you understand them. You pick up their emotions. Sometimes you take on their pain, which is easily done. This is not helpful spiritually, as you then have to transmute that pain through your own body. When this chakra is active, it sends out feelers to another person's emotions. Ask these dragons to help you use this gift properly by assessing what the other person needs, so that you can pour soothing energy into their chakra to raise its frequency.

Solar Plexus Chakra

This chakra is incredibly sensitive and designed to keep us safe by sending out fingers of energy to discover what is happening around us. For example, say a car is travelling too fast near you on the motorway. The chakra warns you to slow down. Or your child is out late. This chakra advises you to put their guardian angel on extra alert. Or you meet someone you find incredibly attractive, so it could be dangerous for your current relationship. Your stomach 'turns to water' as this chakra screams, 'Be careful!' When you call in the aquamarine dragons from Neptune, they funnel their energy into this chakra to raise its frequency. Then you act from the deepest wisdom of your soul and trust that the angels are looking after you and your loved ones. When danger approaches you simply raise your frequency level above that of the situation and your chakra sends a finger of gold to your child to keep them safe. Or it surrounds you in a deep gold light and you are cocooned in safety.

Heart Chakra

When this chakra feels empathy, compassion and pure love towards someone, fingers of light radiate from it to embrace that person. You feel their heart ache. At lower frequencies you may shut down so that you can ignore their pain. Or you may feel impelled to help them in such a way that you interfere with their karma. Ask these dragons to pour their special vibrations into your heart, so that you understand another person totally but can stand back from their emotions. This is what an angel does. This raises the frequency of your heart chakra and the other person's so that they can see their pain from an enlightened perspective and start to release it themselves.

Throat Chakra

The throat chakra is incredibly sensitive. It stands for honesty, truth, integrity, and higher connection. The fingers of light from this chakra check if someone is telling the truth or if another's vibration resonates with yours. It ascertains if it is safe for you to speak your truth and most of us learned as children that it is not, so we close down our light. It is also the chakra of clairaudience, where you hear the voice of your higher self, your angel or another illumined being, usually as a golden thought. When the aquamarine dragons pour light into this chakra, they raise it to the frequency of universal consciousness. This means you attract people to you who accept your truth. This chakra reaches out to the Angels of the Golden Ray. Many rays on different colour vibrations flow from Source. The Golden Ray carries the deepest wisdom, higher love and universal truth. These angels open you up to a higher way of being.

Third Eye Chakra

This chakra in the centre of the forehead is a vast psychic searchlight as well as a crystal ball of clairvoyance. Ask the aquamarine dragons to send a vortex of their energy into it to raise its frequency and open you up to greater awareness and enlightenment, as well as clear seeing.

Crown Chakra

This is the chakra of claircognizance or knowing, at the top of the head, which opens perfectly when you are ready. You can ask the aquamarine dragons from Neptune to use their beautiful energy to ensure the petals reach out from this chakra to the points of universal knowledge so that there is a clear connection.

Your Crystalline Light Body

The aquamarine dragons from Neptune are able to pour liquid light into you. This accelerates the building of your crystalline light body, so that you will be able to carry more high-frequency light in preparation for the new Golden Age.

As they flow gently round you, they light up more of the keys and codes of your true essence. They enable you to accept more of your own divine beauty and bring you soul contentment. They help you open your psychic chakras, so you will experience higher levels of enlightenment and see your world and the universe through angelic eyes.

Exercise to Light up Your Psychic Connections

1. Fill a glass with water and bless it.
2. Ask the aquamarine dragons from Neptune to fill the water with their energy.
3. Pause, and know it is being done.
4. Now drink the water, asking the dragons to light up your psychic connections.

Visualization to Attune Your Psychic Abilities

1. Find a place where you can be quiet and undisturbed.
2. Place a bowl or glass of water, or vase of flowers in the room.
3. Close your eyes and relax.
4. Sense, imagine or see the entire room filled with aquamarine light.
5. A beautiful, gentle aquamarine dragon is floating in circles round you, lightly raising your frequency.

6. It approaches you and sends a vortex of aquamarine light spinning into your sacral chakra, attuning your clairsentience to a higher frequency.
7. It sends a vortex of aquamarine light spinning into your solar plexus chakra, allowing your psychic wisdom to come forward.
8. It sends a vortex of aquamarine light spinning into your heart chakra, attuning you to oneness with others.
9. It sends a vortex of aquamarine light spinning into your throat chakra, attuning your clairaudience to a higher frequency.
10. It sends a vortex of aquamarine light spinning into your third eye chakra, attuning your clairvoyance to a higher frequency.
11. It fills the area above your crown with aquamarine light so that the petals of your crown make clear links in the universe for pure claircognizance.
12. Relax and float in the aquamarine ocean of the cosmos and access your deepest soul wisdom again.
13. Thank the dragons and return to where you started.

Chapter 3

Bronze and Yellow Dragons from Uranus

The bronze and yellow dragons from Uranus have a mighty task and are just starting to work with us here on Earth.

One of their missions is to facilitate sudden change and help people or planets in this universe with the consequences of it. This 20-year period of transformation on Earth is considered to be sudden in terms of cosmic timing. The great shift we are undertaking is a drop in the ocean of centuries.

Everything has accelerated so much that, when they see a number of people light up with a new energy, a cluster of bronze and yellow dragons from Uranus passes over them. For example, if the people have been awoken by the Pink Flame, the dragons take the opportunity to spread the Pink Flame to others in the hope that they light up, too.

These dragons also offer support to those who have gone out on a limb for ascension. One example would be those leaders who undertake to bring in change for the highest good. This is often a lonely, isolated position to take and these dragons are with them to give support. Another would be those brave souls, such as wise women, who in former times dared to heal people. Misunderstood, they lost their lives for standing up for their truth.

Helping the Lightworkers

In current times higher spiritual understanding about the angelic realms, oneness, community, animal communication, natural forms of healing, extraterrestrial life, equality of women, the masculine–feminine balance, acceptance of many kinds of sexual expression and a huge variety of other things, are spreading. It is an unstoppable force, yet there is still much resistance from the old order and the collective consciousness.

Those who challenge the norms and bring about social transformation are often derided and vilified. The dragons from Uranus, while fanning the new and different, are helping lightworkers to stand firm in their convictions. Archangel Jophiel and his angels work with them to strengthen and inspire them. Now the bronze and yellow dragons are assisting the angels.

Dare to Be Different

When I was writing *The Archangel Guide to the Animal World*, I was deeply touched by what I discovered about hyenas, who originate from Uranus and are unusual in many ways, from their body shape to their habits. Their message to us was 'dare to be different.' However humble your position, or however ordinary your life mission, do it your way. Be true to yourself and speak your truth. People will hear you and respect you.

Beings from Uranus or those who have visited the planet or had a soul experience there incarnate here to bring about change. Many are coming in now, but once again the animal kingdom has been heralding the way.

How Do the Bronze and Yellow Dragons Help You?

All dragons are comfortable in themselves and who they are but these wise old dragons are able to help you to accept yourself. If you feel different because of your beliefs, they touch your energy fields with the deep knowing that you are supported. They may only influence you for a thousandth of a second at a time, but eventually this develops into a deep-seated conviction or knowing, within you.

The knowing is important. These dragons work with the luminous, pale golden yellow crown chakra. This is the thousand-petalled lotus at the top of your head. Each petal or chamber is a portal that links to one of God's thousand vibrations.

When deeply spiritual people sing the thousand names of God, it is a profound experience. It opens up the crown chakra and links it to the cosmic crown chakra, Uranus and its ascended aspect, Curonay (coronet). The crown is the seat of gnosis, claircognizance, all-knowing. The bronze and yellow dragons are instruments to help us reach this elevated space.

They cooperate with Archangel Jophiel to help us keep the link from our crown chakra to Uranus and Curonay clear. Curonay has the vibration of divine transformation that brings about higher enlightenment.

Different Vibrations of Yellow

Bronze and yellow dragons carry many vibrations of yellow in their energy fields from the deepest bronze gold to bright sunshine yellow to a high-frequency, luminous, transparent pale shade.

The luminous, transparent pale yellow chimes with the enlightened aspect of your mission, so you see everything from a higher perspective. You no longer regard your difference as a burden but rather as a service of your soul to bring about change or share your truth.

The sunshine yellow tries to spark you with a feeling of happiness or a sense of contentment in yourself.

The bronze gold, that I always see in the wings of these dragons, embraces you so that you have the courage of your convictions. It enables you to stand in your truth and power.

It is a wonderful piece of service work to call in thousands of these dragons to sweep over Earth, spreading the frequencies of the new Golden Age to accelerate change.

Exercise to Bring Self-acceptance

This exercise is very simple, but it attracts these dragons to you magnetically.

1. Go through your wardrobe and gather together clothes in as many different shades of yellow, gold and bronze as you can. If you have no clothes in these colours, you may have to look for yellow tissue paper in various shades and fashion this into a makeshift cloak or garment.
2. Wear your yellow clothes with intention and focus on the bronze and yellow dragons from Uranus.
3. Ask them to bring you self-acceptance, harmony and the courage to be different.
4. Sit or walk quietly in these colours. Sense your aura reflecting the hues.
5. Know that the dragons are working on you.

Visualization to Connect with Divine Vibrations and Know Your Mission

1. Find a place where you can be quiet and undisturbed.
2. Light a candle or find yellow flowers if you can, to energize your connection.
3. Close your eyes and relax.
4. Invoke the bronze and yellow dragons from Uranus and sense or see them approach you.
5. They tell you that they have been watching you from a distance and have passed over you to ignite your inner truth.
6. Sense, feel or see them puffing multi-shaded yellow light into your energy fields.
7. A golden key is lighting up in your crown chakra.
8. The dragons are establishing the portal from your crown chakra to Uranus and Curonay.
9. They are making other links to God's vibrations that you are ready to receive.
10. These beautiful dragons are touching you with a knowing about your mission, as well as self-acceptance, harmony and courage.
11. Breathe it in and surrender.
12. Now invoke thousands of these dragons to sweep over Earth, spreading the frequencies of the new Golden Age to accelerate change.
13. Open your eyes and thank the bronze and yellow dragons from Uranus.

Chapter 4

White-pink Dragons from Venus

Source love is brilliant white, containing the frequency of all colours. This purest white love pours down from Source directly into this universe through a very high-vibration etheric rose. This etheric white and pale pink cosmic rose is the planet Venus, which acts as a transformer, stepping the energy down to a frequency our universe can accept.

The cosmic rose has 33 petals, indicating it holds the Christ light. Venus is known as the planet of love because those who originate from here or have experiences of this planet in their spirit bodies, have wide-open hearts. They have a true understanding of what love is about. They can see the loving hearts of others and expect to be loved in return. Jesus Christ and Lord Kuthumi are two of the greatest examples of beings who have incarnated from Venus.

The white-pink dragons from Venus carry this Source love and the pink of human love. Their mission is to pour their light into the hearts of those who are ready to open their higher hearts.

Like the cosmic rose, your heart chakra has 33 petals or chambers, all of which contain lessons of love that you must learn. Some of these you may have learned in other lives. If enough of the petals are open, these dragons can pour their light directly into your heart centre, rather like sunshine into the middle of a flower. This warms it within so that the petals open. Alternatively, the sunshine can warm the bud so that the petals open. This is how these dragons work on individuals, families and groups. They open hearts to love, but their main intention is to expand hearts to transcendent love.

The Inner Petals of the Heart

The white-pink dragons from Venus work mainly with the last five inner petals of the heart chakra to open you to higher love. Petal 29 is about practising unconditional love and this is a lesson many people are learning now in preparation for ascension. It literally means loving without conditions, while still valuing yourself.

Petal 30 is the lesson of transcendent love that raises your love beyond emotional connection and the physical world.

Petal 31 is about making that connection with the cosmic heart. These dragons, the Angel Mary, Archangel Chamuel and other illumined beings all do their part to help you make this link. Each time you call on them and meditate with them it makes your connection stronger.

Petal 32 opens fully when you experience cosmic love.

The final and most glorious petal, number 33, is about Oneness. Much is spoken of this energy that enables your heart to expand to include all, but when you truly experience it, you truly are a being of love.

Venus

When you talk about Venus these dragons approach you. If you look at a night sky and search for Venus, they will certainly be round you, helping to connect your heart to the pure love energy radiating from the planet.

They work at a higher frequency than the pink dragons and often take over from them to promote ascended love.

Harmlessness, Empathy and Compassion

If you invoke a white-pink dragon, you may be surprised how strong, yet completely harmless it feels. Harmlessness is an ascension quality and it is the essence of these wonderful dragons. If you are developing this quality, call on them, for just having them in your energy field enables you to attune more easily to it. Lord Kuthumi, in his incarnation as St Francis of Assisi, perfected it so that he could have a total rapport with all animals. When you radiate harmlessness you are totally safe for no person or animal feels threatened by you. You become invisible to any aggressors.

Empathy and compassion are fifth-dimensional open-hearted qualities that enfold others in love and healing. To truly own these qualities, you must have self-love. So, ask the dragons from Venus to stay with you and help you to *be* love.

Visualization to Connect with the Cosmic Heart

1. Find a place where you can be quiet and undisturbed.
2. Light a white or pink candle, if you can.
3. Close your eyes and relax.
4. Invoke the white-pink dragons from Venus and sense them flying graciously round you.
5. See or sense them pouring love into the centre of your heart.
6. Feel all the 33 petals of your heart opening.
7. The dragons are creating a shaft of light between your heart and Venus, the cosmic heart.
8. You may sense the higher love pulsing into your heart centre.
9. Bathe in white-pink transcendent love and breathe it in.
10. Merge into the oneness of cosmic love.
11. Thank the dragons and ask them to remain with you.
12. Open your eyes and continue to relax and absorb the pure love.

Chapter 5

Blue-gold Dragons from Mercury

Mercury is the planet of communication and the main task of the blue-gold dragons is to keep connections flowing throughout the universe. On a universal level, these blue-gold dragons act as messengers between the beings on different stars and galaxies. Yet they do more than pass messages – they forge pathways of light, like ley lines, between planets, stars, galaxies and energy clusters. Where there is misunderstanding they puff high-frequency light in to enable beings to reinterpret with enlightened eyes.

They try to do the same with humans but this often proves to be more challenging because most human consciousness is overlaid with karmic patterns that distort clarity of communication. The blue-gold dragons would dearly love to blow this away and enable all interactions to be pure.

They endeavour to keep lines of communication open between nations and individuals. They even help to keep information flowing through the internet, the ley lines and telephone networks.

In the Golden Era of Atlantis, their internet was powered by the Great Crystal. All the information that passed through it was very high frequency, as the people of that time were only interested in spiritual expression. The blue-gold dragons had nothing to do but keep a watching brief. Now they send light through the internet and other networks when asked to do so. However, modern networks are much lower frequency and the dragons cannot raise them because humans are only just becoming ready for something better. When we ask them to send their light along the lines it allows them to send a much greater force, because this is needed to clear out the old.

Telephony

The part of Mercury that has ascended is called Telephony and the blue-gold dragons are tuned in to it. This enables them to focus on helping you to make your communications wise, honest and of the highest frequency. The blue-gold dragons hold integrity and truth in their energy fields and pass these qualities on to you when you are ready.

If you carry a light, they approach you. They are definitely with you, supporting you when you step onto the ascension path.

These air dragons understand the minds of humans. They are aware of the dark blobs in the energy fields that are formed by passionate lower emotions and are, in turn, created by wrong thinking. Despite this, if an individual has integrity and the intention to communicate honestly, the blue-gold dragon will swirl round him and try to assist by blowing away all that is not serving honest interaction. You can ask these beautiful dragons to help you, if this applies to you.

You may have a problem communicating your truth to a relative, a partner, a friend, a colleague or a boss. If you are willing to let go of your ego around it, the blue-gold dragons will power through to enable you to speak with integrity. Their aim is to harmonize relationships by promoting good communication.

Help with Decisions

The blue-gold dragons are small, quick and lively. They energize you. They help you to think quickly and make instant decisions.

They will also help you to move on if you are stuck. First, they will blow away the heavy energies that stop you from shifting. Then they will open up lines of communication to set you free.

Opening New Opportunities

These dragons will also open up new opportunities for you. To do this they will cooperate with your guardian angel. Your angel can arrange synchronicities and coincidences, so that opportunities naturally arise if you are ready for them. Dragons can be more forceful and actively consume energies that block you. They can push you into position to take advantage of a new chance. If you have ever wondered how you got somewhere so quickly, it may be that a dragon pushed you there!

As soon as you commit to higher, purer communication, the blue-gold dragons will come to you. They will pour golden energies into your aura, so that golden angels are attracted to you. When this happens they will all be helping and encouraging you to communicate honestly, so that others totally honour and trust you.

Interplanetary Service Work

Picture the blue-gold dragons connecting the planets, stars and constellations with blue light. See them sending light along the internet waves, raising the frequency of the network round the world. Do the same thing for the television, radio and mobile phone networks. See all the communication networks of the world radiating light.

Exercise to Boost Communication Channels

For this, you will need a quartz crystal.

1. Hold the quartz crystal and dedicate it to higher communication.
2. Hold it up and ask the blue-gold dragons from Mercury and Telephony to touch it with their light.
3. Now place it by your computer or telephone, or place it on a map of the world if you prefer.

Visualization to Enhance Your Communication Skills

1. Find a place where you can be quiet and undisturbed.
2. Light a candle and dedicate it to pure communication.
3. Breathe comfortably and close your eyes.
4. Invoke the blue-gold dragons from Mercury and sense them moving round you.
5. Ask them to clear any karmic patterns that distort your clarity of communication.
6. You may feel or sense them round your throat or your mind.
7. Ask them to blow away any lower energies, so that you are free to communicate from an enlightened perspective.
8. Visualize yourself expressing yourself telepathically and verbally with golden energy.
9. See or sense others responding to you.
10. Ask the blue-gold dragons from Mercury to remain with you whenever you need them.
11. Thank them for helping you.

Chapter 6

Crystal Green and Orange Dragons from Jupiter

These wonderful crystal green and orange dragons bring joy, happiness, prosperity, abundance and success. Everyone needs one! They come from Jupiter with the codes for human happiness in their energy fields, ready to light up your own personal happiness codes.

Happiness is one of the greatest gifts you can possess. It is the best thing you can offer your family. If you are a happy mother, father or child, the family does not feel responsible for their loved one's happiness. What a relief! If a parent who has been unhappy becomes happy, the child subliminally feels the lifting of a huge burden.

Happiness and health are inextricably entwined. As the old adage says, 'Happiness is the best medicine.' It is a stress-buster.

Happiness is a magnetic quality that attracts good. It makes people want to employ you, to choose you as a friend or a partner and it also draws in blessings from the universe. When you radiate this quality, it lifts others up. It even raises those who are stuck in their own lower agendas.

Happiness is gratitude for the gift of this lifetime.

Within the cells of your body and your energy fields is the blueprint for your perfect contentment and soul satisfaction. Some people have impoverished, sick or otherwise challenging lives and yet they glow with an inner radiance. They raise themselves above their condition and choose to see things with eyes of enlightened joy.

The crystal green and orange dragons can light this flame within you, if you are prepared to let go of your old patterns.

Big Dreams

These dragons from Jupiter fly round the universe spreading an ineffable quality of joy to ignite higher hopes and satisfaction. If one comes to you, you inevitably feel lighter.

The part of Jupiter that has ascended is called Jumbay, which means huge, vast and expanded. These dragons also hold and spread this expansive energy. If you wish to grow your business, call on them and they will help you to hold your enhanced vision. For those who want to further their education, this dragon will enable you to find ways and means to fulfil a bigger commitment. If you have big dreams, the crystal green and orange dragons will breathe into you the charisma, hope and vision to succeed.

Never underestimate yourself because, with the assistance of the crystal green and orange dragons, you can achieve much more than you thought.

Abundance

The dragons from Jupiter and Jumbay work with Archangel Raphael's dragons, whirling round people, blowing away poverty consciousness and transforming it into abundance consciousness. Many a person has suddenly felt their heart and mind expand as they unexpectedly conceive of greater possibilities for their career or business. Others have shifted their perception of life when prosperity and good fortune have smiled on them. When these dragons pour the high-frequency, expansive energy of Jumbay into you, your world opens up.

Our Current Time

We are living in a time of development and growth. There may, of course, be local economic, social or political contraction, but the whole world is currently breathing out a great expansive breath. Everything is opening up spiritually in a way that has not been seen since Atlantis. Opportunities and new possibilities are being presented to anyone who is ready to grasp them. And the crystal green and gold dragons are dancing for joy as world progress accelerates. If you are ready to grow, expand and take new opportunities, ask these magnificent dragons to assist you.

Exercise to Draw in Happiness, Prosperity and Abundance

1. Stand outside under the stars, if possible.
2. Call a crystal green and orange dragon from Jupiter to you.
3. Open your arms wide.
4. Say silently or aloud, 'I welcome happiness, prosperity and abundance. Thank you, dragon from Jupiter, for being with me.'
5. Imagine that you and the dragon are standing in a beautiful green and orange portal that reaches up to Jupiter and Jumbay.
6. Breathe in the joyful energy.

Visualization to Expand an Area of Your Life

1. Find a place where you can be quiet and undisturbed.
2. Light a candle to the crystal green and orange dragons of Jupiter.
3. Breathe comfortably and close your eyes.
4. Invoke the crystal green and orange dragons.
5. See them dancing, playing and radiating happiness as they swirl round you.
6. Tell them you are ready to release any old patterns that no longer serve you and you wish to draw in happiness and abundance in their place.
7. Breathe out the old and breathe in green and orange light.
8. Ask the dragons to help you expand any area of your life and sense it happening.
9. Ask them to pour happiness, abundance and prosperity into this area of your life.
10. See it coming into your life and you being so happy to receive it.
11. Thank the dragons.

Chapter 7

Black and Silver-white Dragons from Pluto

These awesome black and silver-white dragons from Pluto are really needed at this time of massive planetary transition. They assist with the destruction of the old so that the new can come in graciously. It is like the renewal in the spring after everything has been prepared underground during the dark winter. Bulbs and buds have been fattening. Seeds have been patiently waiting. Then, when the conditions are right, they burst into the light.

In the same way for thousands of years the planet has been waiting for change to take place on the surface. Much has been prepared in the background. The transition is slow but is gradually happening and the black and silver-white dragons from Pluto are cooperating with the shift. They have been working with Lady Gaia, the angel in charge of Earth, to prepare for the new Golden Age.

Many cosmic portals have opened all over the planet since 2012. The dragons from Pluto swirl round them, as energy is released so that it is integrated into the land and by the people who are ready for it.

Full moons, especially 'supermoons', are pouring divine feminine light over and into the planet. The dragons from Pluto are helping this transformational energy to spread where it is needed.

Since 2015 special ninth-dimensional energies have been attracted to Earth, preparing everyone to raise their frequency. The dragons from Pluto work with many archangels, especially Archangel Sandalphon, to ensure the keys and codes of these energies unlock or light up everything that is being prepared.

The dragons from Pluto also coordinate with many high-frequency beings who are shining their light onto and into the planet. They work behind the scenes and are powerfully effecting change.

Personal Transformation

This is also time for personal transformation on an unprecedented scale. Individuals everywhere are moving onto their ascension path being gently nudged by the dragons from Pluto.

These dragons are well aware of all our subconscious and unconscious processes. They understand our shadow, our fear, our guilt and our shame. As we move to a higher frequency, light shines onto our shadow. Negative things emerge and the dragons from Pluto help us to integrate them. They push us to make positive changes.

Healing Family Patterns

The black and silver-white dragons from Pluto cooperate with Archangel Mariel's magenta dragons to bring about soul healing so that your deepest wisdom can come forward.

At this time of planetary ascension, they are helping to bring destructive family patterns to consciousness. No family is perfect. All have something to work on. Here is a personal example. I had been aware of the destructive effects for years but hadn't worked out the pattern until my daughter pointed it out. I have always been pleased that we are all able to talk and share as a family, but we also shut each other down with a comment or a roll of the eyes. When that happens the shut-down person feels angry and goes quiet. It also stops them from sharing something important or interesting. My parents did this in a big way and it stopped us from being close, right up until their deaths. My children do it to me very occasionally and I was shocked to think I was doing it too but, when I thought about it and watched myself, I realized I carried on the family pattern. We brought it out into the open, discussed it and agreed we would not allow it to happen again. The next day a black and silver-white dragon from Pluto came to me and I wrote this chapter. I realized that this dragon had been instrumental in enabling us to bring this pattern into the light.

Ready for Change

If you are in a power struggle with someone, ask the dragons from Pluto to reveal the true underlying reasons. They bring about slow but complete change. If you are ready to emerge like a butterfly from some situation, know they have been with you throughout the metamorphosis. During this process they can assist with physical changes that take place and with the profound mental and emotional shifts that allow this transformation. These can often be painful. If you are contemplating, dreaming of or reading about the dragons from Pluto they are working on you at an unconscious level and are preparing you for transition to something better.

Secrets

If you are asked by someone to keep a secret, the dragons of Pluto will respect this and will leave it alone. However, secrets are generally destructive, created by shame or guilt. Families and relationships can be torn apart by such a hidden cancer working away below the surface. It uses a great deal of energy to keep a secret hidden. The dragons from Pluto help to bring it to the light so that it can be revealed and accepted.

Countries, corporations and organizations also have aspects they want to hide. Countries that aim to be peacekeepers but whose economy is based on selling arms are an example. A church where sexual abuse is denied and covered up is another. Some of these activities have been rampant for centuries and the dragons from Pluto are working overtime to reveal bribery and corruption of many kinds. They are penetrating many shadows with their light.

We are on the brink of change.

New Beginnings

The darkest hour is before the dawn. There is the pain of labour before a baby is born. And there is often a dark night of the soul before a magical rebirth. The dragons from Pluto destroy the old during the dark time so that the new can emerge into the light of day.

Visualization to Encourage Transformation

1. Find a place where you can be quiet and undisturbed.
2. Light a candle to energize your connection.
3. Close your eyes and relax.
4. Invoke a black and silver-white dragon from Pluto.
5. Sense or see it in front of you and tell it you are ready to reveal to yourself your hidden emotions and concealed patterns.
6. Ask it to shine light into your inner world to facilitate a transformation in you.
7. Be still and quiet for as long as you need.
8. Ask the dragon to shine light onto any family patterns that are holding you back.
9. Be still and quiet for as long as you need.
10. Send an army of these dragons into a country, corporation or organization and ask them to start their work to reveal what is necessary for the spiritual transformation of the world.
11. Thank the dragons and spend some time examining your life.

Chapter 8

Black Dragons from Saturn

Saturn is often known as the planet of restriction and limitation, but it is really the planet of spiritual discipline. The beings from here, including the black dragons, remind you of the spiritual laws of this universe. They only restrict you if what you are doing contravenes them, for this makes your spiritual journey more difficult and also earns karma.

When you adhere to spiritual law, the black dragons from Saturn bring you the wisdom to do what you need to do for the highest good.

St Germain and the Masters of Quichy

The ascended aspect of Saturn is known as Quichy, and these black dragons work directly with the Masters of Quichy, the 12 mighty beings who take decisions for the planet. They encourage you to focus on your ultimate vision. These dragons appear to you when it is time for you to assume, with discipline and focus, tasks that will ultimately lead towards your goal. You are not reading this at this moment by chance.

St Germain, who is now Lord of Civilization, one of the most important offices in this universe, was also Merlin, the magician, in one of his many past lives. He originates from Saturn and has applied himself to self-discipline and understanding the laws of the universe. He has undertaken many initiations or tests to hone his skills, and with the powers gained through spiritual discipline he was able to master the elements, create magic and become immortal.

Plan Your Goal

Once you have decided on your goal – however large or small – the black dragons of Saturn will help you to plan what you are going to do to reach it. At the same time they will encourage you to balance your life. They will assist you to organize yourself, concentrate and focus so that you do everything calmly and in a centred way. These powerful dragons will give you the determination you need to do whatever is necessary to fulfil your mission.

The Violet Flame of Transmutation is held in Saturn. The black dragons carry this energy and when they work with you, they use it to dissolve any of your doubts or thoughts that do not support your vision. This is a mighty gift that they offer you.

Balance Your Base Chakra

We learn the lessons of spiritual discipline in our base chakra, which has only two petals or chambers, the masculine and the feminine, and these must come into perfect balance for this chakra to become fifth-dimensional.

Black is the colour of the Divine Feminine. These black dragons hold you in the peace and calm that allows the magic and wisdom within your soul to develop. However, too much yin (feminine) energy ultimately leads to stagnation. To balance this with yang (masculine) energy, Archangel Gabriel, the pure white archangel in charge of the base chakra, works with the dragons from Saturn to create perfect equilibrium here.

This helps to ground you on your ascension path and ensure you do everything for the highest good of all and totally trust the universe to look after you.

These dragons will often come to you when you have passed a test or initiation for it indicates that you have exhibited spiritual discipline. They ask you to celebrate your success and inspire you with the understanding that your path in life is opening up to something new and better.

Trust the Dragon Cards

The *Dragon Oracle Cards* will tell you which dragons are with you, so trust them. While I was writing about the black dragons from Saturn I heard from Birkan Tore, a psychic who was filming for a TV series in Scandinavia. He had a punishing schedule, visiting places where there had been accidents and tuning in to tell the survivors or loved ones exactly what had happened – really challenging psychic work. This is an abbreviated account of his email about his experience of being helped by water dragons and dragons from Neptune.

He said that while filming, one of his biggest supporters was a black dragon from Saturn, named Sathor. He had a total of 24 cases and would film for three days and be off for two. He did Dragon Card readings daily and he received the Black Dragon from Saturn card on every single one of his filming days. It only showed up on those specific days. It was an amazing validation for him because he would know that his day would go well and he had passed the previous test of seeing the accident or incident that had taken place at each location.

One day he did not get the card and the filming was cancelled. There was no test to pass!

He meditated and asked why these particular dragons were coming to him. They said they could act as a loving coach or supervisor and help people to accomplish tasks and missions that were complex or challenging for them. They help people to stay focused and not be sidetracked or distracted. They keep our energy aligned with the task until we accomplish it.

Birkin added that he did not think he could stay as open, intuitive and focused for so many hours without their help.

Visualization to Help You Focus on a Challenge or Task

1. Find a place where you can be quiet and undisturbed.
2. Think of a challenge or situation you are facing.
3. Invoke a black dragon from Saturn and be aware of its energy as it approaches you.
4. Ask it to restrict you to doing only what is for the highest good in this situation (in other words, according to spiritual law).
5. Invoke Archangel Gabriel and see him arrive in his pure white light.
6. Together they place a perfect black and white yin–yang symbol in your base chakra.
7. Relax and let it integrate into your system.
8. Know that these two mighty beings are guiding you.
9. Thank them and open your eyes.
10. Watch your thoughts and actions as you undergo your challenge for as long as it takes.
11. When it is over, congratulate yourself and do something to celebrate.

Chapter 9

Pure White Dragons from Orion

Orion is the planet of wisdom. Wisdom is about taking knowledge and information, and using it for the highest good of all. Beings from all over the universe come to the Masters of Orion, the 12 wise, enlightened beings who are in overall charge of the constellation, for advice and guidance.

The pure white dragons from Orion carry this special light of wisdom in their energy fields and can help you to see things from an enlightened perspective. They also blow away lower thoughts that come into your head so that the wisest remain.

Knowledge is a function of the left brain, while wisdom is developed in the right brain and the heart. These dragons have the ability to transform all the knowledge you have gained on your ascension path into pure wisdom that accelerates your journey. They help to open your right brain so that you can assess things through your heart.

The White Ray

White denotes purity and being true to your essence. It indicates truth, honesty and enlightenment. These dragons vibrate with these qualities and have the ability to pass them to others.

These wondrous dragons shimmer with blinding pure white light. White holds all colours at the highest frequency. It opens up all possibilities. It allows you to connect with Source light. When the pure white dragons from Orion approach you, many things become possible.

There are many beings who operate on a pure white ray and they are naturally connected with the pure white dragons of Orion. Archangel Gabriel himself spreads his white light of clarity, purity and joy across many universes. He travels with his angels and dragons. The pure white dragons from Orion also accompany him on special missions to hold all that is happening in the vibration of enlightened wisdom. If you ask, one will accompany you when you have something important to do or a special meeting to attend to hold the outcome in wisdom and truth.

The unicorns are known as the purest of the pure for their essence is diamond bright and they vibrate with divine truth. They work with the visions of your soul, so when you ask a white dragon from Orion to hold your dream in wisdom, the unicorns will add their blessing. These dragons may also hand your vision to the unicorns to take to Source to be activated.

The Great White Brotherhood operates throughout the universe and has many strands; for example the Essenes and the Cathars belonged to it.

Serapis Bey holds the pure white Flame of Atlantis and can place it over your aura when you are ready, so that every cell in your body is bathed in flawless, shimmering white light. The pure white dragon of Orion can fan it into life so that for an instant your light flashes across the universe.

All beings who carry white light visit the Temple of Truth. This was set up in the era of golden Atlantis and is now available in the inner planes. In this illumined space it is easier to access the vibration of pure truth and to receive blessings from the unicorns, Serapis Bey, members of the Great White Brotherhood and the Dragons from Orion.

Preparing for Higher Ascension

When the dragons from Orion approach you, you are being prepared for a higher level of ascension as they work through your heart to light up your own soul wisdom. You may find that you are offering heart healing to others with your words of wisdom.

As always you are asked to look at your own thoughts, words and actions with eyes of enlightened wisdom. Are you always operating for the highest good? Ask the dragons of Orion to whisper to you and raise your frequency.

The dragon of Orion encourages you to act with integrity and honesty in all situations. This enables you to develop pure white in your aura so that people trust and respect you. If you ask them to, the dragons will take you to Orion in your sleep or meditation to meet the Masters of Orion. Just being in their presence purifies your essence and illuminates your heart.

Because these dragons work through the heart, with their influence you will find that your own wings of light start to grow bigger and spread.

Visualization to Receive White Light and Wisdom

1. Find a place where you can be quiet and undisturbed,
2. Light a candle and dedicate it to meeting the white dragons of Orion.

3. Close your eyes and relax.
4. Ask Serapis Bey to place the White Flame of Atlantis over you.
5. Invite the dragons of Orion to fan it into a huge flame that lights up your cells.
6. Ride on the pure white dragon's back to the Temple of Truth.
7. Inside the shimmering white temple, unicorns, Archangel Gabriel, Masters of the Great White Brotherhood and white dragons await you.
8. The light is blinding as they bless and illuminate you. Relax in the light.
9. Now the dragon takes you through the dimensions to the White Temple on Orion.
10. Here the 12 wise Masters of Orion await you.
11. You get off your dragon and bow to them.
12. You may hold a question in your mind or just receive light from them.
13. Each one in turn touches your heart and looks into your eyes.
14. Receive the wisdom that is being downloaded to you.
15. Return with your dragon to where you started and thank it.
16. Know that your aura holds radiant white light.

Chapter 10

Blue Dragons from the Pleiades

The Pleiades is a star cluster through which Source downloads blue heart-healing light into this universe. A vast blue etheric rose with 33 petals floats between Source and the Pleiades. It has 33 petals because it holds the Christ light of unconditional love. The blue rose is a cosmic transformer and Source healing light is stepped down through it to the Masters of the Pleiades.

The 12 illumined Masters of the Pleiades are charged to use this cosmic energy for the highest good of all beings in this universe. They reduce its intensity even more before they pass it to those beings connected to the Pleiades, who in turn step the energy down further to a level that we humans can accept.

These special dragons are a beautiful mid-sky-blue colour, the exact colour of Mother Mary's blue robe. Their role is to carry the Pleiadean heart-healing to all parts of the cosmos. They have the wisdom that allows them to use it appropriately, so they prepare you to accept it with great love. This means that the healing light always comes to you at a time and frequency that is right for you. They shower it over you as an act of grace when you are ready to open your heart and receive it.

The Blue Rose in Your Chakras

These dragons can place a shimmering, vibrating blue rose with 33 petals into each of your chakras to activate them with love and healing. When this happens your chakras spin faster and the Pleiadean blue rose is projected out to touch others with its healing energy.

This is what happens to you energetically when the dragons light up your spiritual centres with the healing blue rose.

When these dragons place it in your Earth Star chakra you feel the love of Lady Gaia very strongly and any sense of disconnection is healed. It enables you to ground your life with love. It can also shoot out to touch the Earth Star chakra of others so that they can do the same.

When the blue rose is in your base chakra you lovingly trust the universe to provide for you and keep you safe.

When these dragons place the healing blue rose in your sacral chakra, all past unhelpful beliefs about relationships and sexuality dissolve in healing light and are replaced with warm accepting love.

When it spins in your navel chakra, you welcome all beings regardless of colour, race, culture or religion. The blue rose of the Pleiades heals with such love that all boundaries dissolve.

When the blue rose fills your solar plexus chakra, your fears are healed, so that you are empowered and give others confidence.

When the blue rose is in your heart chakra you heal others through your heart.

The blue rose in your throat enables your words to heal. Your utterances are automatically loving.

If the blue Pleiadean rose is in your third eye the mental healing you emit from here is softened with heart love.

The petals of the crown chakra reach out into the universe. When they vibrate with Pleiadean love you become magnetic to good things.

A Pleiadean rose in your causal chakra invites you to step into the angelic realms with love.

With the rose in your Soul Star healing is taking place for you at a soul level.

The Pleiadean rose in your Stellar Gateway allows Source healing to filter down through your chakra system.

When the blue rose is anchored in your chakras and influences you, you pass this influence to others. A Pleiadean dragon will assist you and this enables the angels of the Pleiades to connect easily with you. Then the beautiful shimmering blue dragons will activate a huge energetic blue rose in your heart, so that you can transfer Source healing under grace to any person or situation.

You become a portal for the Pleiadean healing light and the blue dragons swirl round you.

Exercise to Create a Portal for Blue Pleiadean Healing Light

The more energy and enthusiasm you put into this, the more effective it is. You will need a piece of A4 paper, a pen or pencil and some Blu Tack or blue plasticine.

1. Light a candle and call in the blue dragons of the Pleiades.
2. State aloud or mentally: 'My intention is to be a portal for the blue Pleiadean healing energy. I ask the dragons to support me.'
3. Think about the healing portal as you do the remainder of the exercise.
4. If you wish your physical self to become a portal, draw a stick figure in the centre of the paper.

5. Soften the Blu Tack or plasticine and divide it into 12 little lumps – one to represent each chakra.
6. Roll them into balls. If you wish you can fashion them into tiny blue roses.
7. Now place them on the drawing of yourself in the chakra positions as follows.
8. The Earth Star below the feet.
9. The base chakra at the base of the spine.
10. The sacral chakra above it.
11. The navel chakra at the tummy button.
12. The solar plexus above it.
13. The heart chakra in the centre of the chest.
14. The throat chakra in the throat.
15. The third eye chakra in the centre of the forehead.
16. The crown chakra on top of the head.
17. The causal chakra above the crown.
18. The Soul Star above the causal.
19. The Stellar Gateway at the top.
20. Take a blue crayon and draw the blue light flowing down through your body and radiating out through the blue chakras or roses.
21. Place your creation somewhere it will not be disturbed, such as on your altar, and energize it with your thoughts.
22. Ask the blue dragons of the Pleiades to look after it and activate your healing intention.

Exercise to Make Your Home into a Blue Pleiadean Healing Portal

Follow the above instructions but set your intention as follows. 'My intention is to make my home into a portal for the blue Pleiadean healing energy. I ask the dragons to support me.'

1. Draw your home on the paper. You can use a photograph if you prefer.
2. Place the 12 blue roses in a column down through the centre of it.
3. Take a blue crayon and draw the blue light flowing down through your home and radiating out through the blue roses.
4. Place your creation somewhere it will not be disturbed, such as on your altar, and energize it with your thoughts.
5. Ask the blue dragons of the Pleiades to look after it and activate your healing intention.

Visualization to Connect Your Heart to the Blue Cosmic Rose

1. Find a place where you can be quiet and undisturbed.
2. Light a candle, if possible – a blue one would be perfect.
3. Close your eyes and relax.
4. Mentally invoke the blue healing dragons from the Pleiades.
5. See or sense them shimmering and swirling round you until you feel surrounded by soft blue light.
6. Be aware of them blowing Source healing light into your heart chakra so that the petals open wider and wider.
7. You are aware of a huge blue rose with 33 petals forming in your heart centre, radiating blue light.
8. As the dragons constantly puff more healing blue into it, you notice they are connecting your heart directly to the blue cosmic rose above the Pleiades.
9. The dragons are acting as transformers, ensuring it is a perfect energy for you, under grace.
10. You can radiate what you receive to people and animals, under grace.
11. Relax and continue to receive and send out blue Source healing through the Pleiades.
12. When you have finished, thank the dragons and open your eyes. Notice how you feel.

Chapter 11

Green-gold Dragons from Sirius

Lord Kuthumi, the World Teacher, is in charge of the spiritual universities and training colleges for this universe. These are housed in the etheric realms and are connected to the ascended aspect of Sirius, Lakumay.

Many of these learning establishments are renowned throughout the universes and beings from all parts of the cosmos attend them. Here, all advanced knowledge, spiritual law and technology is taught from a higher spiritual perspective.

The foundation for every spiritual path is balance, to bring the masculine and feminine energy into total equilibrium. This is why these dragons from Sirius are a shimmering green, the colour of natural balance. They also hold incredible wisdom, which is reflected in the gold hidden under their wings.

The green-gold dragons from Sirius hold the energy of education and learning in the highest and purest light. The golden radiance under their wings enables them to shelter pupils attending the spiritual universities. It also allows them to understand and help them in the best possible way, hold them steady to absorb downloads of information and even open their minds, when necessary.

These dragons may well be taking you to these Academies of Light on Sirius during your sleep to advance your spiritual knowledge and understanding. This is to bring universal truths and an understanding of pure love, crystal technology or sacred geometry to your spiritual pathway.

Receiving Sacred Knowledge

The luminous green-gold dragons are much more than protectors or guides. They carry the codes for the illumined path as well as the technology to come forward in the new Golden Age. They impart this to people the moment they are ready to receive and understand it. They will move gracefully round you, downloading streams of information into your chakras whenever there is an opportunity. You must be relaxed and aligned to your spiritual path in order to receive this knowledge and so they often visit you at night when you are comfortable and receptive.

Once you have received this sacred knowledge, you will consciously or unconsciously pass it on to others. So, if you connect with a green-gold dragon from Sirius, you have been selected to spread this special wisdom to others. It is an honour to be a transmitter of sacred knowledge. The great beings of light in charge of our universe will see that you are helping to bring about the new Golden Age.

Teaching in the Universities of Sirius

Our spirits travel at night. Those who are ready do splendid and important work during the sleep state. If you are a lightworker, whether you are aware of it or not, you may be helping stuck souls to pass, healing or counselling people while they are out of their bodies, helping people who are involved in accidents, nurturing those who are afraid or doing any number of other tasks.

You may also be teaching in the inner planes. Your spirit may even be lecturing in the universities of Sirius while you are asleep and thousands of beings from many star systems may be absorbing your light. The dragons from Sirius will be travelling with you and looking after you.

My friend's mother was a teacher during her life and she loved it. When she died her spirit stayed in close touch with the family and within a month she let them know that she was on Sirius, teaching in the inner plane universities and she was really enjoying it. I love to think that everything we learn and do on Earth is used when we are in spirit.

Cosmic Travel

All dragons help you to travel through the dimensions but the green-gold dragons of Sirius are particularly adept at conducting you safely into much higher frequencies. They are also cosmic travellers, who bring spirits from all over the universe to the Halls of Learning. They know how to keep sacred information safe and will hide you under their wings as they travel if this is necessary. They are very protective.

If you aspire to become an Intergalactic Master, you will train with the Seraphim Seraphina in the training schools and these dragons will look after you during your cosmic journeys.

Visualization to Visit the Universities of Sirius

1. Find a place where you can be quiet and undisturbed.
2. Light a candle if possible, close your eyes and relax.

3. Invoke a green-gold dragon from Sirius.
4. Sense or feel it swirling round you.
5. Ask it to take you to the teaching establishments of Sirius.
6. Ride on its back and feel golden light protecting you.
7. Ahead you see white-yellow gates bearing a yin–yang symbol to bring you into balance.
8. The dragon takes you into a vast chamber where there are many students of every shape and colour.
9. There you relax into a chair, breathing comfortably.
10. You are handed a crystal and you hold it to your third eye.
11. Light containing keys and codes of spiritual information and knowledge is downloaded into your third eye.
12. Your aura is lighting up as you receive.
13. When you are ready, get onto your waiting dragon again.
14. Fly together back to where you started.
15. Thank your dragon.

Watch your dreams, as you may bring back memories from your visits to Sirius with the dragons. Also notice any subtle changes in your thoughts and any new ideas that come to you. You may find you are speaking in a wiser, more illumined way. Do this visualization often. It is especially effective if you do it last thing at night.

Chapter 12

Silver Lunar Dragons

Source sends divine feminine light through the Moon into Earth, where it bathes you in its magic and mystery. It contains all the secrets of ancient wisdom, which includes the powers of creation and love.

The silver lunar dragons carry the divine feminine light in their energy fields and their aim is to touch people with its qualities: from cooperation, peace and harmony to creative expression, continuity and sharing, to equality, love, unity and wisdom. Their mission is to bring about balance, so that the yin–yang energies of the planet can harmonize perfectly for the new Golden Age.

They will also bathe you in their shimmering silver light and help you to come into balance. That way you can help the world and all the beings on Earth.

The Moon

The Moon is a gateway between Earth and the constellation of Lyra. In this space these dragons can rest to be energized for their missions. Here, they also connect and communicate with unicorns and different kinds of angels to exchange information and wisdom. Then they stream into Earth, particularly when the Moon is full.

Supermoons

As the frequency of the planet becomes lighter, we are being graced with more extraordinary supermoons. These happen when the Moon is nearer to the Earth than normal and so it appears to be much bigger and brighter. Supermoons are bathing us all in much more high-frequency divine feminine light than we have ever experienced before. No wonder many people are being knocked off centre by this cosmic phenomenon.

When a supermoon shines onto a lake or sea, the body of water becomes supercharged and has an impact on our cellular structure, accelerating the formation of our crystalline bodies. The silver lunar dragons are nudging people to be aware of the moonlight and to go out into it. When you moon-bathe it can dramatically impact on the development of your third eye. It is sensible to respect its power and be careful not to overstimulate your chakras. Ask the silver lunar dragons to protect you and make sure you receive only the right amount of moonlight each time.

The Causal Chakra

Your causal chakra is the pearl-white transcendent centre above your head. It is directly connected to the Moon, which pours its light into this chamber in order to wake it up and activate it. It is often known as your own personal moon and through it you make connections to the higher spiritual realms. When it is ready you meet angels and illumined masters. The shimmering silver lunar dragons circle round it, helping it to light up, become bigger and expand spiritually, so that unicorns can step through it to enter our planet and help us all to ascend.

Exercise at Full Moon to Wake Up and Expand Your Chakras

1. Sit or stand in the moonlight where you can feel it bathing your third eye and your causal chakra.
2. Place a glass of pure, still water beside you.
3. Mentally or aloud ask the silver lunar dragons to clarify and wake up your third eye in a perfect way. Relax and trust they are doing this.
4. Then ask them to light up and expand your causal chakra. See or sense it becoming huge.
5. You may be aware of angels, dragons or unicorns above your head.
6. Relax for a few minutes bathing in the moonlight.
7. Finally bless and drink the water.

Visualization to Light up Your Divine Feminine Energies

1. Find a place where you can be quiet and undisturbed.
2. Light a white candle and dedicate it to connecting with the silver lunar dragons.
3. Close your eyes and relax.
4. Invoke the silver lunar dragons and ask them to bathe you in their energy.
5. Know that the codes of your personal divine feminine energies are being lit up.
6. Focus on your causal chakra and visualize it as a pearl disc above you.
7. Sense the silver lunar dragons touching it, so that it grows into a huge moon.
8. Allow angels, dragons and unicorns to float round and through it.
9. Know that you are closer to the angelic realms than ever before.
10. Thank the lunar dragons and open your eyes.

Chapter 13

Golden Solar Dragons from Helios

Golden solar dragons come from Helios, the Great Central Sun. This is the Sun beyond our Sun and it represents the essence of pure divine masculine energy. The golden solar dragons carry in their energy fields the raw power and force of our universe, the energy of inspired leadership, the strength to move mountains. They never operate in isolation unless mere might is needed, because the masculine must be balanced by the feminine. Masculine strength without feminine wisdom can be dangerous; feminine wisdom without masculine strength is merely ineffective; so silver lunar dragons usually accompany these dragons.

When the golden solar dragons from the Great Central Sun come near you, they touch you with divine masculine energy. In doing so they send a surge of courage and strength through you that you may palpably feel. They also ignite your inherent masculine qualities of confidence, independence, logic, focus, discipline, leadership and assertiveness. The lunar dragons balance this with divine wisdom, so that you are able to reclaim yourself as a peaceful warrior. They enable you to stand in your power with wisdom.

When your masculine and feminine energies are balanced, people feel safe when they are with you. They trust you. It is like having parents that operate in total harmony together for the highest good of all.

Archangel Metatron's Divine Forge

Within Helios the awesome Archangel Metatron creates the light matter that is the foundation of our existence. It enables Earth and all on her to live and experience and grow. It is the forge out of which the new will emerge for the awaited Golden Age. The golden solar dragons carry the blazing light codes for this emergence and ignite all who need to be transformed by this energy.

DNA Reprogramming

Part of this is the DNA reprogramming that is now starting to take place, so that we can step into the next phase of our evolution. These magnificent golden dragons from the Sun are working in balance and harmony with the silver dragons from the Moon to activate our 12 strands of DNA once more. They are helping us to feel safe so that we can trust the universe to look after us and then they can illuminate our cells. Within them all those codes of DNA that have been dormant since the fall of Atlantis can begin to wake up and reconnect. We are being intensively reprogrammed to prepare us for the new Golden Age.

Helios the Stargate

Helios is the stargate between our universe and the Source of All That Is. It opens up an accelerated path through the dimensions to the Infinite. It emits the notes that enable us to fly like homing birds to our ultimate destination. Wrapped in the golden, star-spangled cloak of Helios, we can dance to ascension.

Ask the golden dragons to bring you here in your meditations or sleep and then help you to shimmer up your Antakarana Bridge – the Rainbow Bridge built through prayer, mental discipline, visualization, meditation and other spiritual practices, to link the personality to the soul; the soul to the Monad; and the Monad to Source, using Mahatma energy (powerful golden-white light which heals on every level and can speed up ascension dramatically).

Become a Spiritual Light

When you work with the golden solar dragons of Helios you have the courage to speak your truth and the wisdom to become a spiritual light. You are given the responsibility of leading many into the new Golden Age. You do this by example, living in a fifth-dimensional way.

Exercise to Activate the Light Codes

1. Mentally or aloud ask the golden solar dragons to come to you.
2. If possible, sit or stand and relax with the golden Sun softly bathing your third eye. Only do this at a time when the Sun is warm and gentle.
3. If this is not possible, imagine the Sun shining on and caressing your third eye.
4. Sense the dragons activating the light codes.
5. Feel this spreading through your body, starting to activate your DNA.

Visualization with Archangel Metatron to Reprogramme Your DNA

1. Find a place where you can be quiet and undisturbed.
2. If possible, light a candle and dedicate it to the golden solar dragons of Helios.
3. Sense them surrounding you and attune to them.
4. Ask them to take you to the Stargate of Helios for DNA reprogramming.
5. One of the shimmering golden dragons invites you to sit on its back.
6. Feel its raw masculine power as it thrusts through the dimensions to Helios.
7. You see the vast glittering golden gates of this great stargate to the universes.
8. The gates swing open and you sweep through into a fabulous angel-filled space.
9. When you have become accustomed to it, you see that Archangel Metatron awaits you in blazing orange light.
10. You step off your dragon into a powerful column of his orange energy.
11. Breathe deeply as your DNA starts to be reprogrammed and new light codes are downloaded into your energy system.
12. Remain as long as it feels right.
13. Then thank Archangel Metatron and get back onto your golden solar dragon.

14. Return to where you started.
15. Remember to thank the dragon and rest for as long as possible so that subtle changes can start to take place.

Chapter 14

Orange-gold Dragons from Arcturus

When the orange-gold dragons from the star system of Arcturus come into your life, you know that it is time for you to stand in your power, for you have a destiny to fulfil. This may be in the field of creativity, spiritual leadership, bringing forward technology or healing. If this dragon is with you, be assured that your destiny will serve humanity or the planet. These dragons are very high-frequency beings, totally service orientated, with a desire to help you personally and our planet Earth.

They come to selected individuals, some of whom have shut their eyes, refused to listen and turned their backs in the past. Right now, you are asked to invite these dragons into your energy fields, for this is a new era and it is time to move forward.

Beings from Arcturus

The beings from Arcturus are highly evolved. Their vibration is so high that they have almost become a group consciousness, as the common good becomes more important than individual identity. This oneness is where humanity on Earth is heading and it will be established when we are fully in the new Golden Age. The orange-gold dragons from Arcturus are helping us to attain this aspiration by showing us visions of Arcturus and how they live there. In some ways it is similar to the way of life in the Golden Era of Atlantis except that the beings are etheric and so do not have physical bodies. The dragons constantly inspire us by reminding us of where we have been, where we are going and how much we can attain.

Healing

The Arcturians are known throughout the universe as healers. In fact, they understand how to work with spiritual energies and employ their knowledge to heal your chakras, meridian lines, energy bodies and even your DNA. Give yourself time and space to relax deeply, then call in these dragons so that they can use their expertise to help you. They will ground you, clear your energy body, align you to higher energies, help you absorb them and raise your frequency.

They will also enable you to attune to Arcturus.

Light Ships

Their light ships are very highly evolved. They traverse this and other universes, spreading their light and knowledge. The light ships are also healing chambers where any being can be realigned and 'reconstructed' to their divine blueprint. They, along with the space ships of Commander Ashtar, the seventh-dimensional commander of the Intergalactic Fleet, are part of the security that protects our planet. They destroy lower energies and entities approaching Earth. The Arcturian dragons travel with them, faster than the speed of light.

Absorbing the New Frequencies

Their spiritual knowing can be applied to creativity, technology and all the energies in the universe. The dragons from here carry all this information in their fields and pass it on to those on Earth who are ready. Because they hold the blueprint of our future on this planet, they pass it on to you. If one comes to you, expect them to be lighting up your hidden codes.

In addition, they are very aware that humans are trying to integrate the many high vibrations that are being poured into Earth now. When the dragons wrap their orange-gold energy round you, you find it easier to absorb and utilize these new frequencies. Just call them in and ask them to help you.

The Stargate of Arcturus

Arcturus is a stargate or portal between this universe and others. It also acts as a gateway between dimensions. Many beings who are entering this galaxy receive teaching and healing here to prepare themselves for incarnations or experiences in this plane. You can ask the orange-gold dragons to bring you here for orientation and guidance. Then you will be a guiding light.

Be a Walking Master

The fact that you are reading about and connecting with these magnificent dragons suggests that you are a Walking Master or ready to become one, helping to bring in the new Golden Age on Earth.

Right now, armies of the dragons from Arcturus are flowing together to and round our planet, stimulating great evolutionary change.

You have volunteered or been chosen to incarnate right now, during the most important 20-year period there has ever been in the history of this planet. Because there has never before been a double-dimensional shift like this, light beings are being called on to stand up as spiritual guides, leaders and light bearers. When you do your part these orange-gold dragons from Arcturus will be holding you in their extraordinary light. With their support you can transcend all lower limitations and help prepare the people of the planet for the new Golden Age ahead.

Visualization to Visit the Stargate of Arcturus

1. Find a place where you can be quiet and undisturbed.
2. Light a candle for your connection with these dragons.
3. Close your eyes and relax.
4. Call in the orange-gold dragons and feel one of these vast, light-filled, pure beings beside you.
5. Tell it you are ready to be a beacon for the new world.
6. The dragon looks at you with infinite love and blows an orange-gold light through and over you. You may feel yourself fizzing as you rest in it.
7. It asks if you would like to visit the Stargate of Arcturus and you nod.
8. You find yourself on its back moving faster than the speed of light through many dimensions.
9. As you see the vast orange-gold portal ahead, take a deep breath.

10. Your dragon floats with you through the shimmering gates into a wonderland.
11. There are beings of all shapes and sizes visiting as you are.
12. Your dragon takes you to a healing chamber where you are invited to lie down.
13. A small being stands at your head, manipulating energy inside and around your body.
14. Rest for as long as you need.
15. Your dragon fetches you and takes you to where you started.
16. As you open your eyes, thank it and know something has lit up inside you.

Chapter 15

White-gold Dragons from Lyra

The constellation of Lyra holds a cross-shaped stargate to another universe. This illumined gateway contains twelfth-dimensional Christ light. Although we can now open the door to it, the light within that portal is awesome beyond our current comprehension.

Christ light is Source love and wisdom merged, white being love and gold, wisdom. It is stepped down through different frequency bands for us to access. At the fifth dimension it is gold and this is the level at which we usually experience it. However, since 2012, more people have accessed it at a golden-white seventh-dimensional level.

In 2015 a portal opened to Lakumay, the ascended aspect of Sirius. Here, the Christ light is held at a ninth-dimensional frequency in a white-gold globe that we can now reach when we are ready.

Archangels Christiel and Mallory (the angelic Keeper of Ancient Wisdom) look after the Stargate of Lyra, which leads to a portal protected by white-gold dragons. The twelfth-dimensional Christ energy held here is pure white, the vibration of God, containing all the frequencies of love. It is the highest-frequency Christ light.

Unicorns

Many unicorns and dragons wait beyond the Stargate of Lyra for us to draw them to Earth through magnetic resonance. These include magnificent golden-horned ninth-dimensional unicorns, who also carry the highest frequencies of pure white Christ light. When your causal chakra blazes a bright enough light, the angelic gatekeepers allow them to enter this universe. Archangel Christiel sends a stream of silvery white light down through the Moon, allowing the dragons, as well as the unicorns, to access the energy fields of Earth. These illumined beings finally step down into Earth through the causal chakras of ascending humanity.

The dragons of Lyra protect the unicorns and conduct them on their journey. They are able to do this because they hold the element of fire as well as air. Unicorns are of the element air.

DNA Repatterning

The keys and codes of light that Archangels Christiel and Mallory are now allowing through this Lyran stargate will bring about the new patterning in our DNA to prepare us for the crystalline bodies we will inhabit when the new Golden Age is established. This will enable us all to carry a much higher frequency. It will free us to be self-healing entities again and to activate spiritual technology more advanced than anything created in the Golden Era of Atlantis.

One of the tasks of the white-gold dragons of Lyra is to help us access the codes within the light from Lyra without burnout.

The Causal Chakra

The white-gold dragons of Lyra are helping with the development and illumination of the causal chakra. This is a vast chamber of peace and stillness above our crown, that holds the divine feminine qualities and is our own personal moon. These dragons protect it for us.

This chakra is the space through which we connect to the higher dimensions of the spirit world. It is our gateway to the angelic kingdoms of fairies, angels, dragons and unicorns. Through it we also access the Illumined Masters, other evolved spirits, the Lords of Karma, the Intergalactic Council and pools of divine energy.

As soon as we are ready a new world opens for us.

Ninth-dimensional Christ Light

Remember that you already hold Christ light within you. It is your divine birth right, placed there when your original divine spark or Monad left Source. So, your task is to activate this, your inheritance from God, and these dragons will be delighted to help and guide you, if you ask. When you request help from the dragons with pure intention, it is always forthcoming.

Look out for the clues, which may be words you overhear, something you read, a message on your phone or a slogan on a lorry. It could be anything.

Listen to their promptings, which seem to be your own beautiful ideas or concepts. The dragons (like angels) may drop in a thought that you should drink more pure water, or go to bed early and ask them to help you, or walk in a certain place, or take a day off work or meditate about them. The suggestions they make for your highest good are endless.

Remember that the Christ light contains the light of the Sun and the Moon, divine masculine and divine feminine, in perfect balance.

Ask the white-gold dragon from Lyra to take you to the ninth-dimensional pool of Christ energy held in Lakumay, the ascended aspect of Sirius. Ask them to do this in meditation or while you sleep. Make sure you relax as much as possible, so that your cells can open and absorb the energy. Visualize yourself bathing in the pool, which shimmers and swirls with pure love and light. Feel yourself absorbing all you are ready to receive.

When you return, continue to feel the white-gold light in your aura and practise pure unconditional love in your daily life. Your aura will radiate the incredibly high frequency of white-gold, while the white-gold dragon from Lyra will support you by continuing to pour Christ Light into you. Take time to find a quiet place where you can listen to its wisdom and guidance.

Illuminating Your Ascension Path

These dragons also help to illuminate your highest possible ascension path. Their light is so luminous that when they rise above you and open their wings, it is as if a searchlight is shining onto the path in front of you. Because their frequency is so different from ours, you may not be consciously aware of this but your soul will know!

Exercise to Absorb Christ Light

This exercise could not be simpler.

1. Run a warm bath.
2. Get in and relax in the water.
3. Ask the White Gold Dragons of Lyra to fill the water with the highest frequency of Christ light you are able to absorb.
4. Imagine the white, gold and yellow light soaking into the cells of your body and notice any higher thoughts or ideas that flow through your mind.

Visualization to Activate Your Causal Chakra

1. Find a place where you can be relaxed and undisturbed.
2. Light a candle and dedicate it to the white-gold dragons of Lyra.
3. Close your eyes and really relax.
4. Be aware of a beautiful luminous white-gold dragon in front of you.
5. It invites you to ride on it and you find yourself on its back.
6. Together you float through the universe until you see Lakumay in front of you.
7. Here there is a great ball of the brightest white-gold light you have ever seen.
8. The ball opens and your dragon floats in and sits beside a pool of shimmering Christ light, surrounded by flowers.
9. You descend from the dragon and lie in the pool.
10. Birds are singing to you of your divine magnificence.
11. Your dragon opens its wings and glorious golden light, like sunshine, illuminates you.
12. You surrender yourself, relaxing your feet, calves, knees, thighs, tummy, solar plexus, chest, shoulders, arms, back, neck, face and head in turn.
13. When you are ready the dragon brings you back to where you started.

14. It breathes into your causal chakra above your head and you can feel this getting bigger and brighter.
15. At last you imagine yourself stepping through your causal chakra into the higher spiritual realms. Here, you receive blessings from the angels, unicorns, masters and dragons.
16. Rest until you are ready to open your eyes.

Chapter 16

Dark Blue Galactic Dragons

The illumined dark blue galactic dragons are vast ninth-dimensional beings. They sparkle and shimmer with the golden cosmic wisdom that they have earned through aeons of higher service throughout the universe.

They glide among the stars, planets and constellations, harnessing and absorbing their celestial light for use on their divine missions. As they do so they balance the keys and codes of information within the light.

Stellar Destinies

Stars, planets and constellations have their own destinies. Although the beings in those planes do not have free will and must follow spiritual law, they can either just exist or they can exist gloriously. The dark blue galactic dragons attempt to bring about the latter, so that every star and the cosmic beings connected with it can develop their divine potential.

Beings in Other Planes

Etheric beings inhabit the universe. They are a variety of shapes and colours and on different frequency bands from us.

As Orb photography became more popular, I was amazed at the pictures we were being sent of beings who had allowed themselves to be snapped. The first one I saw was a blue being from the Pleiades, who had no rigid shape but was more like a cloud. The colour blue was the exact colour of the Pleiadean rose I had visualized. Many beings from other planes show themselves to us as we expect to see them. The dark blue galactic dragons help to coordinate the variety of beings in this universe. They also impart cosmic information and wisdom to any entity who is ready and open to receive it. This includes humans on Earth. By sharing and spreading light these dragons are helping to promote universal oneness and higher ascension.

Becoming an Intergalactic Ambassador

As you embody this illumined wisdom, it opens you to higher possibilities, especially if your soul cherishes a wish to be an Intergalactic Master. The deep blue galactic dragons work with Seraphina, the Seraphim in charge of the intergalactic schools of this universe. You can attend these in your sleep if you are ready and your soul wishes you to do so.

You are ready when your 12 chakras are open and active. Then, you access your Antakarana Bridge, the Rainbow Path to Source. You progress along this path by undergoing many initiations. However, as you step onto the Antakarana Bridge, the path divides into two and you are offered a choice. One is to progress directly to Source. The other is to progress via Seraphina's training establishments and learn to serve as an intergalactic ambassador. Neither path is superior, but they are different. You do not consciously make a choice because this decision is taken at a soul level. If you are in intergalactic service, the dark blue dragon will connect very easily with you. If you are interested in the spiritual workings of the universe or if you are fascinated by this dragon, you are quite possibly already attending the intergalactic schools during your sleep. You may even already be an Intergalactic Master whose spirit is teaching and illuminating others from this planet and other planes of existence.

Your Soul Journey

Since your soul left your Monad you have travelled and experienced existence throughout the universes. In order to incarnate on Earth your soul must be at least seventh dimensional. This is because this planet is considered to be one of the most challenging places to explore and navigate without getting severely contaminated. Also, once you have been here, you are karmically attached to this planet and must return again and again until all karmic cords are dissolved and there is nothing to draw you back.

Although your soul is at least seventh dimensional, when your personality self passes through the Veil of Amnesia, human thoughts and emotions push you down, often into the third dimension. Since 2012 lightworkers have been endeavouring to bring themselves and everyone else into the fifth dimension. As human consciousness everywhere rises, new-born babies will be able to maintain their innocence.

The dark blue galactic dragons are able to beam a ninth-dimensional cosmic searchlight into your Master Blueprint to ignite the codes that contain the seventh-dimensional light and mission of your soul. This helps you listen to the Voice of the Universe.

The Voice of the Universe

The Intergalactic Council is a body of 12 illumined beings who take the decisions for this universe. They are supported by a vast assembly of beings, many from different parts of the cosmos and some still in physical bodies.

The Intergalactic Council works in cooperation with the Karmic Board, consisting of 12 beings who administer the karmic laws. Some beings serve in both capacities.

The Intergalactic Council and the Lords of Karma receive guidance from a higher authority, the Voice of the Universe.

Visit the Intergalactic Council

If you are ready to serve the planet and the universe the dark blue dragons will take you, during your sleep or in meditation, to visit the Intergalactic Council. There are other beings who can conduct you on this elevated journey, including Archangel Butyalil, the pure white universal being who helps with the flow of the cosmic currents.

When you enter the temple where the Intergalactic Council meets you can make requests for the betterment of humanity, the animals and the planet. Since 2015 humans have been allowed to make a personal supplication as long as it is for the highest good of all. It is a great honour to present such a petition, so give it thought.

You can also contribute your ideas and energy for the smooth ascension of the world. After all you are in a physical body on Earth and experiencing life in a way that the members of the Council cannot.

As you stand in front of the Council, the dark blue galactic dragon is pouring his light into you to keep your frequency as high as possible. You may communicate telepathically with the members of the council or their advisors. They may raise their arms and invite the Voice of the Universe to speak. Relax, listen and be ready to serve. Whatever wisdom you receive may be of life-changing importance. Whether you realize it or not, you are now serving in a galactic capacity.

Visualization to Meet the Intergalactic Council

1. Find a place where you can be quiet and undisturbed.
2. Light a candle to raise the frequency and invoke a dark blue galactic dragon.
3. Close your eyes and relax.
4. You may become aware of a huge dark blue dragon approaching you or it may contract its size and make itself smaller for you.
5. As you connect energetically with the dragon, be aware of a light starting to beam from its forehead.
6. The light touches you and ignites the codes of your Master Blueprint.
7. Relax and breathe deeply, knowing that something is lighting up within you.
8. The dragon invites you to sit on its back and together you fly through the universe.
9. It is taking you into the highest dimensions of this universe to the temple where the Intergalactic Council meets.

10. You find yourself standing in the courtyard of a magnificent temple surrounded by 12 illumined beings.
11. Your dark blue galactic dragon is holding you in a beam of light.
12. If you wish, you may present a petition for the betterment of humanity, animals or the planet or for the highest good of your own life.
13. The Council hears your petition. They may raise their arms and invite the Voice of the Universe to speak.
14. Listen carefully.
15. The members of the Intergalactic Council bow to you and you return the bow.
16. Now step back, get back onto the dark blue dragon and return to where you started.
17. Thank your dragon and know you will travel again together in your sleep.

Chapter 17

Alpha Dragons

The huge alpha dragons radiate an incredible deep, shimmering, black colour. Internally, they hold Archangel Metatron's blazing golden-orange-white light at its highest frequency. They can create and they can destroy. They can manifest and de-construct.

Creation and manifestation need a fusion of masculine and feminine energy. The alpha dragons work in balance and harmony with the omega dragons to provide the perfect yin–yang balance to build our world.

These powerful and magnificent dragons participated in the creation of this universe and especially this planet. With Archangel Metatron they provided the divine masculine power that helped thrust the stars and planets into the manifest world. While the omega dragons nurtured the vision for Earth held in the mind of Source, the alpha dragons breathed life into it. They shaped the original planet and they are coming back close to Earth again as a new phase in the development and growth of our planet approaches.

Where the old needs to be destroyed, the alpha dragons are working with the elements to ensure it happens according to the divine plan. They are with the fire dragons when volcanoes erupt, with the earth dragons when earthquakes rumble, tectonic plates move or avalanches are precipitated. They are working with water dragons when tsunamis or tidal waves rise; and with air dragons helping with hurricanes, gales and tornadoes. The Alpha dragons help carve out the new outlines and shapes of the mountains and the land. They create new countries, islands and continents. They were instrumental in the destruction of the various experiments of Atlantis and in the rebuilding of the new land mass each time it rose again. And they will continue to do this wherever necessary to shape the land as required for the new Golden Age.

Not every island or country is destined to participate in the approaching sixth Golden Age on this planet. Some places will be submerged under water, giving the land time to be cleansed, while land masses will be thrust up to be inhabited. The alpha dragons will carve out the new according to the fresh blueprint.

However, we humans are co-creators, as we manifest with our thoughts and visions. Where we focus light the alpha dragons can strengthen and underpin fault lines. Where we focus negative thoughts, the Alpha dragons can destroy land if it is not pure enough. We are having a powerful and important impact on the planet and these dragons are watching our thoughts. They also work with the collective mind of humanity, because this has great power when it is ready to bring something new into being.

The alpha dragons only ever work for the highest good. They are here to facilitate the deconstruction of all the things that no longer serve Gaia. And they are helping to construct the new golden world at a much higher frequency than we enjoy now.

Creation in Your Personal Life

When you have pure intentions and a project or wish that you are ready to create, call in the alpha dragons. With their powerful, raw masculine energy, they can give you strength to go forward with your vision. At the same time, they breathe their power into the materialization of your personal vision.

Visualization to Help Shape the New World

1. Find a place where you can be quiet and undisturbed.
2. Think of the new Golden Age approaching. For the highest good of all, what is outdated on the planet and needs to be destroyed? What needs to be created afresh? (You may like to consider the physical demolition of certain buildings where ugly things have happened, or outmoded transport systems. And the creation of high-frequency systems throughout Earth, beautiful buildings or the shoring up of fault lines etc.)
3. Call an alpha dragon and watch its sinewy black shape appear in front of you.
4. This etheric being is inviting you to step right into its centre.
5. You step through the skin into its glowing golden-orange-white inner.
6. You are illuminated and inspired. Breathe in the golden-orange-white light and feel the power inside you.
7. Picture your vision for the new world so that the alpha dragon can see it in your mind.

8. Travel inside the vision to the place you wish to see transformed for the highest good.
9. Watch the alpha dragon breathe in the old structure, then breathe out the new creation.
10. Focus your energy into this work, too. See the new construction radiating golden light.
11. Thank the alpha dragon and know you are helping to usher in the new Golden Age.

You can also do this visualization for a personal creation that is for the highest good of all.

Chapter 18

Omega Dragons

These beautiful yet gentle white-silver dragons carry the divine feminine vibration of creation. They were part of the incredible team of light beings who worked with the vision for Earth before it was even birthed and have been connected with us ever since.

They contain the energy of Shekinah. This is the extraordinary high-frequency feminine creative force that nurtures the visions of Source. The Seraphim sing the concept to the omega dragons and they start the process of making it physical. As above so below. As in Heaven so on Earth.

The Golden Era of Atlantis offers a perfect example of how the masculine and feminine energies of creation worked together in a fifth-dimensional way. At that time, when a couple married they would meditate for the kind of soul they could best serve. Often the extended family would meditate with them. One or more souls would respond and one would be chosen. The physical sexual act between the parents would provide the explosion of energy and emotion to draw the spirit of that soul down from the unmanifest world to be conceived. The mother would nurture the foetus, give birth and continue to look after it infant.

In exactly the same way, the masculine and feminine energies are needed to work together to conceive and manifest an idea into physical reality. The alpha and omega dragons take the visions of Source and the higher dreams of individuals and groups of people and cooperate with them to bring about the best possible outcome.

Shekinah is also the feminine equivalent to Archangel Metatron's high-frequency masculine light and they work together. So since 2012 the omega dragons have been liaising with Archangel Metatron to birth the new higher consciousness coming to Earth now in preparation for its new Golden Age.

Birthing a Vision

The beautiful white-silver omega dragons collectively hold the vision for the new Golden Age with Lady Gaia. They see the divine intention for the evolution of our planet and, while this is being birthed, are trying to support and nurture us in the best possible way.

The omega dragons can see into those minds that are clear and focused on a vision beyond their little self. So, they are looking for and connecting with individuals and groups who have a special idea that they wish to birth for the benefit of others or who are holding the vision of a better future for humanity and all beings on Earth.

These ephemeral dragons want to help you if you have a wish for yourself that will also assist others or the world. Your dream starts with a picture. The omega dragons blow energy into your mind to fan the picture to spread the new higher-consciousness light.

If one of these dragons comes to you or you find yourself thinking about an omega dragon, ask it to look into you to find the greatest desire of your soul. It is time to give birth to a special new project, pathway or aspect of yourself that has previously remained hidden. Let the dragon enfold you and your project, and nurture you in the

Divine Feminine, so that you can hold your vision and bring it to fruition in a wise, balanced and harmonious way.

About Shekinah

Shekinah is a 10th-dimensional universe of love and joy beyond our current comprehension. The creative, high-frequency divine feminine energy carried by the omega dragons is held here and they return to this place for rest and recuperation before they slide down through the dimensions again to work with us.

Many spirits from the universe of Shekinah have incarnated to help the planet move forward. For the majority of them this is their first incarnation, which is quite a challenge. While they carry pure light in their essence, most of them have a very difficult incarnation, because they simply do not understand the mindset on Earth that produces human behaviour. They may become quite third-dimensional until they access their wisdom and their light switches on again. The omega dragons are naturally drawn to them and help them where they can.

Visualization to Help You to Birth Your Vision

1. Find a place where you can be quiet and undisturbed.
2. Close your eyes and mentally wrap yourself in a sparkling white-silver energy.
3. Feel this sparkling white-silver light shining out into the universe and drawing a white-silver dragon to you.
4. Feel the love and pure light emanating from this

dragon.

5. Ask it to look into your heart, mind and soul and see the greatest vision and potential that you hold there.
6. Let it take the seed from within you and fly with it through the dimensions.
7. Watch it approach the wondrous Seraphim surrounding Source.
8. See it hold up the seed to be activated and blessed by them.
9. Picture that seed sprouting and growing as the white-silver dragon carries it back down through the dimensions.
10. The beautiful dragon stands in front of you and blows the sprouting seed through your heart into your soul.
11. Feel a spark of hope within you becoming a blaze.
12. Know that the Omega dragon will continue to nurture and help you look after your vision.

Chapter 19

Source Dragons

When Source dragons come to you, you are truly blessed for they are of the highest-frequency white with almost transparent wings. They attune you to All That Is, to the Cosmic Oneness, to the Infinite. They call on you to centre yourself and be still, so that you can enter the silence and wonder of the mystical worlds beyond our comprehension.

They remind you that there is a spark of illumination in the centre of all the dimensions, galaxies and universes. In this infinite point of pure stillness and love is the Heart of Source, from which flows unimaginable light and sound. This is the Godhead, surrounded by the Seraphim who sing the Will of the Creator out into the universes within the vibration of Ohm. This is radiated out at a frequency beyond the sight, sound and comprehension of humans in a physical body.

The shimmering, transparent Source dragons take the intention of Source and step it down to a frequency we can access. They coordinate with the Seraphim and the cosmic angels.

When your will and your wishes align with the divine will, the Source dragons light them up with the mystical flame of creation to bring them into physical reality. If your desires are not tangible, for example if you truly, deeply want to serve in a particular capacity, they will help your light to blaze out so that your path of service is noted. Then angels are dispatched to you to prepare you to embark on it.

So, what if your wish is pure and passionate but is not in accordance with the divine blueprint that was set out for your life? This rarely occurs for we are surprisingly tightly guided and inspired on our pre-chosen path. However, this is an example of what might happen. Say you have been a politician in several incarnations and your life plan was to be born into a political family where you would remember the skills and reawaken a desire to serve your country or local area. Then you had a teacher at school who lit the flame of creativity in you. You decided to be an artist. This is your free will so new information is fed into the great universal computer and many lives are changed as a result of it.

A Source dragon works with you to attune you and your new pathway to the Infinite. It brings you different notes or sound vibrations from the Seraphim to harmonize your new life choice. It breathes them into your heart and you may feel them.

In this century, for the first time in aeons, we have been set free to choose many different careers, relationships or adventures in one incarnation. Source dragons are diligently retuning us. They are portals of light, through which we can keep our divine connection, especially when we make profound changes in our lives.

I have met many people who have changed their given names, in other words they are calling new energies into their lives. The Source dragon helps them to retune to their new destiny.

Breathe

All sentient beings breathe, for the intake of oxygen is the connection to Source. If it is cut off, you no longer exist as a physical entity. If you pant-breathe or take shallow breaths, you feel anxious because your link to the Creator is more tenuous. On the other hand, when you breathe deeply your bond to the Godhead is much stronger and you feel safer and more contented.

The Source dragon can work with you more closely if you breathe deeply, meditate and enter the silence. It will actively help your meditation practice if you ask it to.

The more you remain centred, still and calm, the more smoothly your life flows, as this dragon is keeping you connected to Source. And when you are centred in the moment, you can listen to the silence. You can also maintain beautiful and positive thoughts, so you are automatically creating a grace-filled future. Be prepared for the sacred to enter your life. Expect magic.

My Story

When I had colon cancer I was seriously ill. I was in and out of hospital for weeks sprouting tubes in all directions and slept much of the time. When I was awake I would focus on my breath and visualize my new garden filled with colourful flowers. It was an intensely peaceful time for me because I had to centre in the now.

At the time I was not aware of the Source dragons round me but when I had recovered I asked them if they had been with me. They replied that they always take every possible opportunity that is presented to attune people to the Godhead. And because I remained so still and centred with a calm mind, they were able to pour divine light right into my consciousness. They showed me a picture of a raging torrent and said that many people's thoughts were turbulent like that, so if they tried to pour in pure white, liquid light it was immediately dissipated or distorted. If a mind was like the mirrored surface of a calm pond, high-frequency light could be gently floated in.

Higher Psychic Attunement

Birkan Tore told me that he always tunes in before starting work for the day and asks for angelic assistance. He told me that after he received his *Dragon Oracle Cards*, he tuned in and asked which dragon or dragons would like to work with him that day while he read for his clients. For two consecutive weeks, every morning he drew the Source Dragon card. He texted me, 'As you know no matter how talented the reader is, the information that'll come through will be defined by the frequency of the intuitive. The higher they vibrate and the more aligned they are with the Source, the better, more accurate and helpful information they will bring through.' He added that the Source dragons align psychics and intuitives to Source energy and have become an important part of his daily centring process.

They will also align those who ask them to, not just psychics, so it is helpful to everyone to call on the Source dragon as a daily routine.

The Source dragon is a mighty loving force and it helps to build your Antakarana Bridge to Source. This is the connection from your Stellar Gateway, built through many initiations and learnings, up to your Monad and Source. It accelerates your ascension.

Visualization to Connect You with Source through the Chakras

1. Find a place where you can be quiet and undisturbed.
2. Picture the Cosmic Diamond around your energy field.
3. Breathe slowly and comfortably three times into each of your 12 chakras, concentrating on your

breath as you do so.

4. Start with the sparkling silver Earth Star chakra.
5. Next, breathe into the platinum base chakra.
6. Now move on to the shimmering pink sacral chakra.
7. Next breathe into the glorious orange navel chakra.
8. Now it's the turn of the deep gold solar plexus chakra.
9. Next breathe into the pure white heart chakra.
10. Move on to the powerful royal-blue throat chakra.
11. Now breathe into the transparent crystal ball with a hint of green in your third eye chakra.
12. Next, the transparent crystal yellow crown chakra.
13. Now breathe into the moon-white causal chakra.
14. Move on to the bright magenta Soul Star chakra.
15. And, finally breathe into the vibrant, golden-orange Stellar Gateway.
16. You are now grounded, open and aligned.
17. Invite the Source dragon and sense it alighting beside you in a flash of transparent white.
18. Feel the purity of its light.
19. Ask it to bring a thread of pure white light down through your Antakarana Bridge from Source to your Stellar Gateway.
20. Then bring the thread of pure white light down through your chakras into your third eye.
21. Feel your mind become totally calm, like the mirrored surface of a still pond.

22. Sense or feel your consciousness attune to the Infinite.
23. Thank the Source dragon and open your eyes.

Conclusion

A vast array of elemental dragons are here en masse to help you to ascend. You only have to think of one and it will be with you. You may not see or hear it because it is on a different frequency from you, but you may sense its presence and notice the effect it has in your life.

Your personal dragon loves you and is waiting patiently to connect with you. There is also a wise, open-hearted and highly evolved dragon to help you in every situation and with every aspect of your life. Do you need to be more grounded? Ask the earth dragons to help you. Do you want deeper love or romance or heart healing? Invite the pink dragons to touch you with their gentle energies. If you are dedicated to ascension, call on the appropriate dragons to help you to expand your higher chakras and protect your journey.

Whichever area of your physical, emotional or spiritual life you wish to develop, don't hesitate to call on the dragons to assist you. They are devoted, loving and compassionate. They offer tools to enable you to walk your journey more swiftly and easily.

All these glorious and beautiful dragons are facilitating the great move to ascension. They have helped me enormously and I do hope you will connect with them and allow them to fly with you on your personal journey.

Image Download

To download images of some of the dragons who have stepped forward to be included in this book, please visit www.hayhouse.co.uk/downloads and enter the Product ID and Download Code as they appear below.

Product ID: 17
Download Code: Dragons

For further assistance, please visit www.hayhouse.co.uk/contact

ABOUT THE AUTHOR

Cheryl Zimmerman

Diana Cooper received an angel visitation during a time of personal crisis. She is now well known for her work with angels, Orbs, Atlantis, unicorns, ascension and the transition to the new Golden Age. Through her guides and angels she enables people to access their spiritual gifts and psychic potential, and also connects them to their own angels, guides, Masters and unicorns.

Diana is the founder of The Diana Cooper Foundation, a not-for-profit organization that offers certificated spiritual teaching courses throughout the world. She is also the bestselling author of 30 books, which have been published in 28 languages.

f angels.dianacooper

www.dianacooper.com